The Contessa Chronicles

A New Vision of Heaven and Earth

by Laurie Beth Jones

The Contessa Chronicles

Cover Design: Shelly Shepherd and Laurie Beth Jones
Cover Illustration: Shutterstock
Interior Design: Fusion Creative Works, www.fusioncw.com

Print ISBN: 978-0-616-00288-9

Published by Laurie Beth Jones, Inc
Version 1.1

Printed in the United States of America

In my dream,
the angel shrugged and said,
"If we fail this time,
it will be a failure of imagination,"
and then she placed the world
gently in the palm of my hand.

("Imagining World" by Brian Anderson)

In Praise of Wisdom

"The Lord formed me from the beginning,
before he created anything else.
I was appointed in ages past,
at the very first, before the earth began.
I was born before the oceans were created,
before the springs bubbled forth their waters.
Before the mountains were formed,
before the hills, I was born—
before he had made the earth and fields
and the first handfuls of soil.
I was there when he established the heavens,
when he drew the horizon on the oceans.
I was there when he set the clouds above,
when he established springs deep in the earth.
I was there when he set the limits of the seas,
so they would not spread beyond their boundaries.
And when he marked off the earth's foundations,
I was the architect at his side.
I was his constant delight,
rejoicing always in his presence.
And how happy I was with the world he created;
how I rejoiced with the human family!"

Proverbs 8:22-31 New Living Translation (NLT)

Prelude

Fia hiked along the dusty trail calling out for Joshua. Her dog had run far ahead of her as they made their way along the canyon rim. She hiked a lot these days, hoping each step would take her further away from the grief that had engulfed her forty days ago. "We will just have to take things one step at a time," her father had said as they all sat at breakfast, trying to ignore the empty chair where her brother used to sit. Nissi. She remembered his smile and him calling out to her, "Let's go for a swim!" Nissi. He was no longer there. Only she and her parents and Joshua lived here now...in this new place far away from where they had been before.

Tears stung her eyes as she thought about him. She wasn't watching where she was going. The land that looked like it stretched out for miles suddenly just stopped.

Fia took one step forward and realized too late that there was only air beneath her. And that is how she found herself falling on this clouded day.

Nothing she reached for held her. After slipping and sliding past sagebrush and boulders, she landed with a thump at the bottom of the canyon, her right leg buckled under her. "Ow," she moaned, rubbing her head, where a knot was beginning to form. She reached down to feel her ankle and was relieved that there were no bones sticking out and no damage other than a few scrapes and bruises. She was grateful her backpack still had some marshmallows in it, as they had helped cushion the blow.

She stood up and winced in pain. "Joshua, where are you?" she called, but this time her voice echoed. She looked up and wondered how she was going to climb back up the cliff, especially with a bad ankle. Her cell phone didn't work out here—something she had been grateful for in the beginning. But now she wished they weren't so far out of range—hadn't moved so far away. Her parents had bought this land only a month ago. She was relieved when they finally packed up the van and left the constraints of their former life. None of them had been the same since her brother died.

Nissi. His name shot through her again like lightning splitting the sky. Then two words stung and engulfed her again.

"Swept away."

Nissi had been playing along the western bank of the river with other boys. She didn't like him to go down there all that much. She thought the water was too swift. But Nissi had said he was a good swimmer, and certainly he was.

So it was a tremendous shock when one of the boys came scrambling up the bank, calling out for her. "Fia, help! It's Nissi!" She dropped her book and had started running as the boy continued sobbing. "Some kids from the other side of the river started fighting and one of them fell into the water. Nissi jumped in to save him, but instead he got swept away. I tried to grab him, I did," cried Peter, who was by now howling with tears.

Fia barely heard anything he said after that. All she heard was "swept away."

She shouted for help, and soon her parents and some neighbors ran down to the river. Some men jumped in downstream from where he had fallen, and others raced along as far down as they could, trying to see if they could save him.

But Nissi, her brother, her source of laughter and fun, was gone. From that day on she had lost her voice. Once confident and strong, she now began to speak only in a whisper. The grief had simply become too much to bear.

Every detail came flooding back.

There had been a giant raft race scheduled for the next day. Instead the ashen-faced mayor called it off, saying the city's resources should be used to find the missing child. Volunteers came from hundreds of miles away and began to sweep the river. The Army Corp of Engineers cut the river's flow to less than half. It had been running at ten feet deep at its height. They cut the flow to less than four.

Helicopters hovered overhead. Mounted sheriff's posses rode out along the river banks. For three solid days they searched, and then the officials called it off.

Fia and her distraught parents and friends met privately with the mayor. "What if he were your child?" they implored. "Could you sleep knowing he was somewhere out there?"

The next day the mayor said he had made a mistake. He called the searchers back out again, saying he did not want family and friends searching the river unaided.

It was a volunteer, a mother walking the bank with her children, who found him. She spotted the red shirt he had been wearing. Nissi's body was caught up in a fallen tree, resting there as if being held, while the muddy water rushed past him.

Fia suddenly leaned back against the embankment, feeling the grief kick her in the gut again as she remembered.

She had actually wanted to go back later, and touch the fallen tree where they'd found him...maybe thank it somehow. Had it known that her brother was dying? Had it fallen deliberately years before so it could be there to catch him…to stop the thunderous river from pummeling him when he could struggle against it no more? Had it deliberately cradled him in its branches until the mother found him? Had a night bird called out to comfort him as he lay there alone, the first night and the second, and finally the third?

More memories flooded through her. She remembered the police chaplain being called...the roads being blocked off and the media trucks zooming up with lights blazing. The next day, the photo in the papers showed a young boy's body wrapped in a white sheet, being carried away on a stretcher.

That was the last image they saw of him.

Her mother was so distraught she couldn't even attend the funeral. A memorial service was held at the school, and students and teachers wept, saying how loving and fun Nissi had been.

Her father quit his job and was gone for a few days. When he came back he announced, "We are moving to a place I found out of town. Pack up your things. We leave tomorrow." Fia had felt relieved when they packed up the van and moved to a place removed from their former life. Her father had wanted them to be as far away as possible from every site that brought back memories. That is why the desert hills had seemed so appealing, and why she had been out hiking them, until she fell.

There is nothing like pain to bring focus back to the present, and Fia was in pain. Her ankle was throbbing. Her head ached as if it had been hit by a sledgehammer. She had landed at the bottom of a deep, narrow canyon, and she decided to make her way through it, hoping it would open up eventually or at least lead her to a place that would offer her a view of where she really was.

She found a tree branch and grabbed it to use for support as she limped along. Wincing with every step, she suddenly came around a corner, and saw it…water tumbling from the rocks above her, cascading down like a shimmering sheet of glass.

She gasped at its beauty. "Oh, wait till Mom and Dad see this," she thought, beginning to feel a little better.

As she looked into the waterfall, she noticed an opening behind it.

She held her breath, stepped through the shimmering liquid wall, and found herself in a cave. "Helloooo," she called out, moving slowly into it—wanting to warn any residents who might not relish the thought of an intruder. She reached down to pick up a rock to toss into the darkness. This would help her see how deep the cave really was, as well as alert any snakes that might be coiling nearby. The rock made no noise at all. "Maybe I need a bigger one," she thought, and she walked a few steps further in, reaching for a stone about twice the size of her hand. When she knelt to dislodge it, her hands touched instead a package caked with dirt. Wiping it off, she carefully unraveled the twine wrapped around it, and out fell an old leather journal.

"I wonder whose this is?" she thought. She took the journal in her hands and turned to its first fragile, yellowed page. As her eyes slowly became accustomed to the light, she sat down and began to read.

▪ ▪ ▪

Part One:
THE RANCH

Chapter One

Dear Diary,

I can't say exactly when I was born, because I can't remember ever *not* being. It seems I was always here at this place we call The Ranch. Sometimes it seems I can go forever without writing much, but some unusual things have been happening here, so I decided to write them down.

Skinner has a lot to do with it, but I will get to him later.

Just so you get a sense of things, let me describe the Ranch and my family to you. The Ranch has every sort of terrain you can imagine and stretches further than the eye can see. It has pink cliffs rising above lush green meadows, and beyond that are rolling hills with little green bushes spotting them. The further north you go you see ever deepening forests, and south is what the Ranch Hands call the Badlands, though I never go there. I prefer to stay around here, where there is beauty everywhere.

Our house is a white, two-story home with a pitched roof and a wide covered front porch. There is a large barn about a hundred yards away with corrals all around it. Farther off, there is a tool shed, and beyond that is the library and art studio, where my mother and father spend most of their time.

My father, "Al," is big and tall and has a voice that rolls over you like thunder. His skin is the color of the earth, and his hands are huge. Sometimes I feel like he could hold the whole world in them, and I tell him so.

Meg, my mother, has eyes that are bright with laughter, and her mind is full of very big thoughts. She is always thinking of something new for us all to do.

When Mom and Dad are together, sometimes there is a humming sound. They look at one another and laugh and then disappear for hours.

My brother Jess and I look so much alike the Ranch Hands think we must be twins. However, Jess claims he is taller than me. We measured one day out at the barn. I stood on tippy toes and even wore my boots that day. Jess got the measuring stick from the tool shed and marked it off and said, "Keep growing, Tess, and someday you'll catch me." "How about now!" I yelled, and grabbed for his shirt. Jess laughs and then we are off, racing down the road. We like to run a lot. Mom told me one time she wanted us to grow up in a place where there was lots of room to run, and nothing but wide blue open skies, so we could lay on our backs and dream.

The house where we live is a very large structure with hardwood floor in some places, polished stone in others. There are floor to ceiling windows everywhere. "Let there be Light!" is one of my father's favorite phrases.

The living room has a huge fireplace made of stacked stone, with leather sofas and chairs surrounding a handmade center table. It was one of Dad and Jess's first carpentry projects together and it is massive and strong.

My bedroom looks down over a private garden, with honeysuckle vines climbing over a wall, spreading their sweet scent around. I have rosebushes of sunset colors blooming all around. As I write this, sitting in the garden, little white fluffs of cottonwood seeds are floating in the air, dancing their way down to the ground.

Yesterday as I sat and did my morning journaling, a hummingbird flew right up to my face and hovered just a moment, as if to say "I see you!" and then zoomed away.

(My mother, Meg, probably set that up.) She loves to leave little love notes under my pillow, or arrange for something special to happen during the day to let me know she is thinking of me.

Mom comes in every night and combs and brushes my hair. I lean my head back and close my eyes and feel as if I am floating. Sometimes she will sing. "Although alone, you can do all. Yourself unchanging, you make all things new." The words come in bits and pieces, as she just hums and brushes my hair, with me counting out loud…fifty-six, fifty-seven, fifty-eight. I love these quiet times with her. I almost always fall asleep before she gets to one hundred.

▪ ▪ ▪

Mom is more magnificent than words can describe. Her eyes are the color of the sea, sometimes cobalt, sometimes turquoise, sometimes azure, sometimes cerulean. I know all the names of blue, and that there are many more kinds of blue, because I spend so much time with her in the Studio. It is a place just beyond the garden, where she goes daily to paint and create. I remember the first time I went in there, I stood with my mouth open like an 'O'. Each color dab on her palette was actually pulsing. She would touch one gently, and it would lift itself off and hover, humming. She would touch it again, and it would pour itself into whatever she had sketched or drawn. The day I was with her she had sketched a plant that was almost as tall as me. She placed blooms on it of pink and burgundy, each with an open face, each pointing out towards me like a trumpet. "Holly hocks I shall call them," she said. "They are proud little bursts of color."

Mom doesn't spend all her time there. Her passion you might say is gardening. Due to her efforts and diligence we have a garden unlike any other. Parts of it, acres of it in fact, provide much of the food we consume. Mom is a vegetarian and doesn't like eating things that have a face on them. "Go vegan," she is always telling Dad. "You'll last longer." He just says "humph" and continues eating his barbecue sandwich.

Before she planted the seeds for everything, she and Dad designed them. The two of them meet every evening, just as the sun is starting to go down. They walk together in the twilight out to the Idea Lab, and sit with their sketch pads on drafting tables. They take big sheets of graph paper and write down formulas with numbers and small letters and all sorts of geometric forms. In the morning they take us out to see, sometimes, what was created the night before. One of the most intriguing creations for me was ants.

Mom said, "We were talking about how something needed to clean up under the picnic tables after the Ranch Hands leave. I certainly don't have time to do it." Dad laughed. "She wanted this crew to be so small they will hardly be noticed. They would need to be task-oriented and organized. When their work was done they would disappear into the earth, so as not to detract from the garden. So I just sat down and sketched it out." "His original design had eight legs instead of six, but I picked up on that and said, 'Well, sometimes we need a filter, too, to catch things that fly,' so I created the spider. It can spin its own silk and come out of nowhere and curl up into a ball." They delight each other like this nonstop.

Jess and I have specific chores around the Ranch. Jess spends lots of time with Dad in the tool shop, making things like tables and chairs. I spend time with Mom in the studio designing things. In the evenings before the sun goes down, we walk the vineyards together, checking out the grapevines, pruning back ones that aren't growing. Jess is also responsible for the sheep, a task he takes very seriously. I am involved right now in helping Mom with the garden, improving its fruitfulness.

Sometimes Dad takes me out on the wagon with him, especially at harvest time. He yells "All hands on deck!" and everybody works long into the night, gathering the sheaves of wheat, then separating the chaff. Jess said one time, "We don't have enough workers," and then Dad said, "Well, go get us some." Jess said with a smile, "Maybe I will," and then we headed back to the house, tired but happy at the same time. We take our boots off by the door and then go inside.

One of my favorite times at the Ranch was when we were little and Mom would bathe us and then dry us off with a gentle wind from the garden. Then Jess and I would both run into the Living Room where Dad was waiting, sitting in his overstuffed chair. He would open his arms and we'd take our place, Jess on the right, and me on the left. Then he would tell us stories, of a land long, long ago as well as times to come.

One night when I was patting his face with my hand, he took it in his and started kissing my fingers one by one. When he got to my little finger he said, "See that moon at the top of your fingernail, just near the very edge?" I looked at it closely and he said, "That was the way the sky looked when you were born."

Then he turned to Jess. He took his ring finger on his right hand and pointed to the tip of its fingernail. "See that really, really big star shape right there?" Jess leaned in, and Dad said, "That is what happened the night you were born. That was a very special night too." Then he hugged us close and rocked us to sleep in his chair. All this took place while Mom did her knitting and darning of socks. "Darn these socks!" she would say. I could hear Dad chuckle and then they both would slowly rise and carry us to bed.

▪ ▪ ▪

Dad took us to learn how to swim one day, when we were very little. He walked with us in his arms into the water at the Lake, going deeper and deeper, and taught us how to float, and tread water, and swim back to shore, making moves like the otters. Once, the wind kicked up and Dad just looked at the waves and told them to settle down, and his voice settled us down. One day, many months after lessons, Jess called out "Daddy, look at what I can do!" He jumped out of the boat we were in and just kept on walking. Mom clapped her hands and Dad smiled at him. As for myself, I stayed in the boat. No need to frighten the fish unnecessarily, I always say.

Everything on the Ranch would be just about perfect if it weren't for Skinner. He is the Ranch Foreman. He also happens to be Dad's favorite worker, but Jess and I don't care for him at all. Jess told me once, "Skinner is up to no good," and I had to agree.

Like one time when I was writing in my journal, I heard someone calling me outside. "Tessa, come here. I have a present for you!" I emerged, blinking from the sudden change of light, and saw Skinner standing across the way, leaning on a fence post. His jeans were pulled low and his hair was slicked back and his shirt was half unbuttoned. His shoulders always look funny to me, perhaps because lately it seems he is trying to disguise his wings. He binds them and straps them down. He wants to look more like us, I guess. To me, the package doesn't work at all.

I heard from one of the workers that Skinner sometimes just stands outside Mom's studio, especially when Dad is away. They say he just stares at her for hours. I think something must have happened once between them because when his name comes up at dinner, Mom quickly changes the subject. She won't even speak his name.

Lately, Skinner has been slinking off when I know he should be working. I see him off in the distance, huddled under the tree in the pasture, and I can't help but get the feeling he is not alone.

■ ■ ■

Skinner Ponders the Studio

Skinner stood and pondered the studio from afar. Creating things had never interested him. He mostly liked to rip things apart. That's how he got his nickname. He was always the first one to volunteer to separate skin from bone. His real name was Mentir Oso – not that it mattered much around here since nobody was really concerned about formal names and titles, at least not as much as he was.

He wore the tag "Foreman" proudly on his chest even though Jess and Tess challenged him on it. "Why do you care so much about labels?" Tess asked. Then Jess added "Dad says your boot tracks will say more about you than any title you can claim." Skinner had no reply to that. They just looked at him, then at each other and the two of them went on their way, like they always did.

The thing that galled Skinner the most was them – that family. When you really got down in the dirt with it, it was that he wanted Meg. He had from the very beginning. It wasn't just that he wanted to take her – to satisfy the need below his belt – it was that she had too much power. Al preferred her ideas over his – and that needed to change.

This union – this co-creation as it were – made Skinner's skin crawl. He had to do something to end their reign of trust – her creativity – her power – her being so almighty.

He'd put his head down and think about it – day after day – night after night, lying in his bunk. He mentioned it to one of the Ranch Hands. EZ Lee Swayed was his name, though everyone just called him EZ.

Skinner bit into an apple one day as they were standing out under a tree. He said he didn't think he could take it much longer –

watching everybody be so happy. He needed to do something to stir things up. In fact, he knew he could run this Ranch differently.

EZ nodded and spit in the dirt. "I'd like to go along with you on that ride," he muttered. "You need a hand with anything, you let me know."

Then at last Skinner could smile. He knew he was not alone.

▪ ▪ ▪

Skinner and Dad used to cook together not so long ago. Skinner designed an oven that got so hot it would incinerate anything it touched. Mom walked in, took one look at it, and said, "That thing is going to hurt somebody."

After that, Dad had Chattanango and some of the other Ranch Hands take it way out back. Skinner asked him if he could have it and Dad said, "Yes, as long as you put it to good use."

Skinner got an anvil and started making chains from the flames, one link after another. He was obsessed with them. Dad and I walked out to check on him one day and Dad asked, "Skinner, why are you making those? We don't need any chains here. We never use them." Skinner kept pounding away, saying, "Just passing the time, Boss, just passing the time."

▪ ▪ ▪

Chapter Two

When I watched the workers hauling away the incinerator at Mom's suggestion, I realized that Dad always listens to what Mom says. He told me once, "Mom chooses the work that I do." "You have that same power, Little One," he said, tousling my hair, "and so does your brother."

Jess especially loves to help with getting all the ingredients together for the family meal. He was amazed the first time he saw how yeast can make bread rise. Now he says he still cannot get over how just a little bit of something can change the whole lot of it. "I don't trust anything that can generate that much hot air," he said, and from that time on he refused to eat puffy bread. He personally left the yeast out, just to see what happened, and it turned into all sorts of things—flatbread, pita bread, crackers. He also is a big fan of honey, so one day he added honey to the mix, and then took it out the back door to share with the ducks and geese and chickens.

Jess cannot stand to see anyone or anything go hungry. One of the rules on the Ranch is that we don't eat until all the animals are cared for, so I am glad that Jess is so faithful about it. He gets up really early to do that.

Meanwhile, however, we all have work to do. Some of us like it more than others. One Saturday afternoon we came into the kitchen and there was a note for Dad on the table in Mom's handwriting. It said, "Honey, I finished off the dishes you left in the sink. You can find them in the fireplace."

I think it was shortly after that they decided to assign Q to help out around the house, including doing laundry duty. Q is one of the littlest workers and is very restless all the time. His one desire is to take on more tasks so he can earn points for the Triple A team (the three A's stand for Angels in Art and Architecture).

This is the group that figures out dimensions and structure and sustainability and visual delight. Some are architects, some are mathematicians, some are scientists and artists and graphic designers and structural engineers. It is a very strict group with high work standards. Only a few workers qualify. And nobody wants to qualify for that group more than Q.

The Q is short for QV, which stands for "Quo Vadis," meaning "Where are you going?" This name suits Q perfectly, as he is always searching for something.

Even though he desperately wants to be in the Triple A group, he can't yet qualify. His problem is twofold, I guess, in that a) he works in the laundry, sorting dark clouds from light, and b) he doesn't always do a good job at that, being unable to distinguish light from dark. He often mixes the dark clouds with the light, and we end up with a hazy mixture that seems to promise rain, but never actually gives it. Dad is particularly displeased with this, as he says "Q, at the Ranch everything must keep its promise." So Q returns with his head down to the laundry, to try again.

One day I found Q moping around, and I said, "Q, maybe what you need is a little more information about the situation," (which is one of Mom's favorite phrases).

"And where would I find that?" Q asked. His shoulders and little wings were still slumped behind him, but he was beginning to sit up a little straighter. "Let's go to the Library and research it together, Q. I will help you."

With that, we made our way through the garden, past the corrals, and headed up the steps to the Library. Mom had designed this building in the beginning. It has seven columns and twelve steps. It is an incredible building made from marble and acacia wood beams hauled in from the east. Sunlight pours into it from the rounded cupola.

We opened the massive door with the Ray of Hope Jess had once given Q telling him, "Never give up." When we stepped inside, we were both amazed at the activity there. There were Ranch Hands unloading Books of Deeds and another group writing out Worker Request Receipts. Off to one side, near a window in the corner, sat the two weavers. I said hello to them. Coen handles the "warp" part and Sydence handles the "woof." They looked up at me and smiled. They were always chuckling over their work. "Oh, won't that be clever," Sydence mutters, and Coen nods and laughs "Look at this!" as they weave their daily threads. "Coen/Sydence" is what they call themselves. They are known for merging textures and colors that never looked like they would go together. Yet somehow, their designs work. Dad and Mom keep them very busy, meeting with them on a daily basis.

As Q and I turned the corner we discovered Dad and Jess were already there. Dad was running his hand down a list and Jess was nodding silently. When I asked them what they were doing Jess said, "Dad was just showing me some names I need to know." Then he stood up to leave. He smiled at Q, ruffled his wings, and started to head out the door. "Some of us have WORK to do," he whispered in my ear as he walked past us. I laughed and waved him away. "You do the manual labor, and leave the invisible things to me!" I called out. Dad just looked at us and smiled.

"What brings you two here today?" he asked, moving over to one of the ladders. "Q has decided to learn more about his condition," I said. "Ahh, research and inquiry. One of my favorite activities," he smiled. "Well done, Q. Because you have asked, I will answer." He pointed to a book high on a shelf above us. "I think you will find what you are looking for in there." "A Brief History Before Time" read the cover. Q got it down, said "Thank you" and flew out the door, knowing there was a lot of study time ahead for him that night.

▪ ▪ ▪

Skinner and the Forge

One of the things Skinner had observed on the Ranch was that nobody ever signed anything. There seemed to be a total disregard for the ownership potential of putting your name in writing on something, whether it be a fence post or a book in the library. He felt this was a major loss of opportunity and had brought it up directly to Al one day. He said, "Boss, I think you should develop your very own brand, and start putting it on everything that you own." Al said, "Why would I want to do that? Everything here belongs to all of us." Skinner said, "But what if something should go beyond the boundaries and somebody tries to steal it?" "Steal it?" asked Al. "What is that?" Skinner said, "Well, it's just a concept, but it could happen that somebody would try to take something that was yours and pretend that it was theirs." Al had just looked at him and said, "Skinner, I don't know where your mind goes sometimes. I would be much happier, and you could get a lot more work done, if you put the concept of 'owning things' away, and head on down to the forge, and start making some tools we really can use around here."

So Skinner went down to the forge and began to play with this concept of theft. As he turned it this way and that another facet began to emerge. What if you could not only take something that belonged to someone else and call it yours, but you could also take something that was really yours and make people think it was somebody else's? Like Al's? Or Meg's? The possibilities seemed endless.

He thought about it a lot in fact. These ideas were forged in hammering metal and shaping it in a fire into something it had not been before. He invented a mark that was invisible to all but the practiced eye.

One day Skinner revealed the instrument to EZ. "We can stick this on whatever we want to, and then when others quickly scan it, it will read as ours, and we can claim it as our own."

If you turn it this way," he continued demonstrating, flipping it upside down, "we can take something we have and make others believe it came from somebody else."

"Why would we want to do that?" asked EZ. "Sounds like we would just be robbing ourselves."

"Ahh, EZ, don't you get it?" asked Skinner. "We could create all sorts of interesting drama around this tool."

"What are you gonna call it?" EZ asked, hitching up his britches.

"I was thinking of calling it 'forgery'," said Skinner with a smile.

▪ ▪ ▪

Chapter Three

About a week later, one of the Ranch Hands came running into the Library and said, "We need you out here quick!" We all rushed out the door, with Mom meeting us at the steps.

Michael had caught Skinner out by the weather station, with his hand around the angel Tierra's throat. She was leaning back against the wall looking wild-eyed and wounded. Her delicate layers of ether were torn, and black smoke wafted from the tendrils of her hair. Her entire body was shaking and trembling, and the only sound she could make sounded like the intense groans of icecaps melting and collapsing into the sea.

"What happened here?" bellowed Dad. "What have you done to her?" Skinner stepped back and said, "I thought I had dominion over her. Isn't that what it means to rule? I wanted what she had, and I took it," he said, with a matter-of-fact air. He looked her over slowly once again. "She is indeed 'firma' I have to say. I'm sure she'll recover," he added, stubbing out the carbon ash with his boot. "I may be the first to use her, but I'm sure I won't be the last."

Dad looked at him, and through him, and now saw him for what he was. "Skinner, I once loved you as my own, and because of that I will not destroy you. But you have offended us—offended her—beyond all decency."

"Get out." He said it quietly at first. He motioned to the Ranch Hands Mike and Gabe beside him, who stepped forward with eyes blazing. "Get out," he said again. Skinner looked over at Mom, who pointed to the Gate and shouted, "Now!"

▪ ▪ ▪

Skinner Leaves the Ranch

"Get out!" He couldn't believe he had heard those words…him, the most beautiful of them all, at one time the beloved. The blood surged in his neck as he strained against the sudden heaviness of his wings. Once his crowning glory, he detested them now. Quickly surveying his means of escape, he began to lighten his load. He reached for a feather on his right: Honesty. That one had to go.

It was the longest feather of them all. Then Humility. Kindness. Decency. One by one he yanked them out, hoping the sudden weight of them would fall from his shoulders as he plucked and discarded the feathers. At last he stood naked, alone. He shook the remaining spines of his wings and pulled them tightly into himself. There could be no wasted time or motion. He had to get out now.

He eyed the hole at the foot of the Gate, licking his lips at the challenge before him.

He fell to his belly, arms at his side, and began to crawl under, away.

EZ also dropped down and followed. His wings, which had never really grown in all the way, were easily scraped off as they both slid through the hole.

A sudden flash engulfed them all. What was done, was done.

▪ ▪ ▪

Things were very somber after that for a while. Dad began walking off alone, sometimes for long stretches of time. When I asked Mom where he was, she just said, "He's thinking."

So we all were thrilled when Dad came rushing into the house one morning, slamming the door behind him. "Come on everyone, you've got to see this!" he said, as he grabbed Mom by the hand and pulled her out the door.

We half ran trying to keep up with him as he practically galloped over the hill. We were headed on the path to his workshop, so it had to be something he had come up with on his own.

Just as we rounded the corner, a huge round head peeked over at us. Its giant green eyes blinked one or two times and then it began to raise its neck—higher, higher, higher. Dad called to it and said, "Come here, Dinah," and the creature walked slowly into the sunlight. We were simply amazed. It was of such a size that it blocked the sun.

"What do you think?" Dad asked. "Isn't she grand?"

Mom gulped a moment, wanting to be supportive. "Well, she certainly is big."

"What is she going to eat?" I asked.

Jess whispered to me, "And who is going to clean up after her?"

Suddenly, there was a snuffling snort and a high-pitched scream in the workshop. Dad turned and said, "Uh oh," as another creature, smaller in size, with big gleaming teeth and little tiny claws, emerged from the workshop. "That's Rex. I'm still working on his arms," Dad said. "I think they need to be a little larger…" Just then the smaller creature squealed an even higher-pitched sound and took off after Dinah.

Dinah was big, but she was fast. She took off running down the lane, over the woods, and into Mom's garden — smashing a season's worth of tomatoes and vegetables. She reached down and yanked up a bunch of lettuce and then headed off again. "Rex, Rex, come back here!" we could hear Dad shouting as he took off after both of them.

Meanwhile, Mom was surveying the ruination of her garden, not at all happy about it. Overhead we saw a giant bat-like creature with huge, pointed wings. It too was flapping toward the woods, blocking out the sun with its size. "I knew we shouldn't have left him alone that long after he lost you-know-who," she said.

Suddenly there was an explosion. The ground shook and the sky filled with a mushroom cloud of smoke and ash, way off to the east of us. Mom and I started running and came upon a scene I will never forget.

Jess was comforting Shalomar, the weather angel, who said, "I don't know what happened. I was working at the controls when suddenly I heard this crash and something huge just knocked me flat."

She was shaking her head while looking at the destruction of the station. She kicked around the twisted control panel and said, "This isn't good." Jess turned to see what she was pointing at.

We stood under what remained of the roof, watching sheets of red ash fall down.

And then I saw them. Out in the field, just beyond us, Dad was kneeling over Dinah and Rex's bodies. Tears of amber flowed down his face as he wept over their remains.

Mom went over to comfort him, and Jess and I decided they needed some time alone. So, we did what we do best. First we walked slowly, and then as we came over the rise, we couldn't help ourselves and raced to Crystal Lake.

▪ ▪ ▪

Chapter Four

I am usually faster, but this time, Jess beat me. He ran down the edge of the pier and yelled, "Tessa, watch this!" He gathered himself into a ball and made a huge splash into the lake.

"Jess," I yelled, "Don't you ever think about giving the fish a little warning that you're coming?" "Nah, they like me!" he assured me. "They even come when I call them." "They do not," I said. "Yes, they do. Come closer, let me show you." I was looking down and just then he splashed me. "Come on, Tess, the water is warm. Jump in!"

"No thank you," I said. "I am going where things are a little more quiet."

"Tess, if you don't talk to me, I'm going to make even the rocks and trees call out!" he yelled. Jess was always saying stuff like that. Sure enough, the crickets would start chirping, and a chorus of sound would arise.

I tended toward the quieter, less showy relationship with creation. Like the fish. I didn't have to catch them or put coins in their mouth or have the wind and water obey me, like he did. (Mom had told me that Jess needed to be able to do these things, as some day he would need them. She told me that I had special gifts too, which would become useful to me in time.)

When it came to the elements, and creatures, I wanted to observe them, and be one with them, and watch how they moved.

I dropped to the edge of the grass at the lake and got very quiet. I moved over where I could see my reflection. The water was so still. But I looked beyond my reflection, as Mom had taught me to do. I saw minnows darting to and fro. I saw waving plants at the very bottom, doing their perpetual swaying dance. I was counting the minnows when suddenly I saw a vision of two very angry faces.

One had raised a rock and was about to smash in the head of the one underneath him. I pulled my head back in shock. Then, suddenly, a rock thrown in the water caused the ripple to wash the vision away. I sat back wondering what I had seen. I wanted to tell Jess about it later.

Just then Chattanango gave us the signal it was time to go back home. As it turns out, I forgot to tell Jess what I had seen. Maybe I should have mentioned it sooner. Maybe things would have turned out differently.

▪ ▪ ▪

One of the happiest days of my life was when Dad and Mom gave me a very special gift. I remember it like it was yesterday. A big cloud rolled in, full of flashing light and thunder, and hovered just outside my room. Dad bellowed, "Tess, come out here. There's something your mother and I want to give you." I put my book down and ran outside, shielding my eyes from the lightning that was just before me. Suddenly out of the cloud emerged the most beautiful creature I had ever seen.

Her neck was arched and her mane flowed down like a wave as she pranced right up to me. She lowered her perfectly formed head for me to pet her, her nostrils flaring and showing a hint of red. I pulled her head close into my chest, letting my hands glide up under the arch of her mane. She smelled like the earth after it has rained. She smelled like new mown hay out in the field. I looked over at Dad and Mom. "She's all yours," they said with a smile. "Now you are really free to roam."

"I will name her Espiritu," I cried. "She is like the Wind!" I leaped onto her back, leaned forward, and we were off at the speed of light.

Her hooves pounded the earth in time with the racing beats of my heart. I leaned as far down on her neck as I could and kept saying, "On girl, on!" I guided her easily with a slight shifting of my weight. It was as if we were one being. She flew over fallen trees and past fences that hadn't been mended.

Finally we slowed to a walk. Espiritu continued to snort and prance, lifting her hooves up high, eager to eat up the ground again. We were now out among the giant cactus…their long arms reaching out to the sky in sometimes poetic, sometimes comical ways. It was so cold now you could see puffs of breath as we both exhaled. Snow had fallen on the mountains all around us.

The only sound was her breathing, and mine. It made me to want to frame this moment forever. I felt like together we could go anywhere, leap anything. With her as my companion, I truly could be quicker than any motion.

Suddenly, I noticed a white tip of a tail. Thinking it might be a deer, we drew closer and noticed a little black dog. Its tongue was hanging out, and it seemed tired. He was so glad to see us he barked and barked. I got off Espiritu as she lowered her nose to inhale his scent. He sat down and raised his paw. "Where did you come from, little guy?" I asked. He just grinned and sat there. I picked him up and laid him over the withers, balancing him just so in front of me. With that the three of us headed back to the Ranch.

When I came riding in with the little dog in my lap Mom rushed out to meet us. "Oh, you poor thing," she said. "You must be very hungry!" She took the dog into her arms and headed to the kitchen. "I'm over here, Mom!" I said. "I know, Honey. Welcome back," I heard her echo as she disappeared inside. I could hear her talking to him softly saying, "What were you doing wandering out in the wilderness like that?"

Jess was not in a good mood when I saw him. He was sitting on the porch swing, rocking back and forth. In fact, he looked mad. "What's the matter with you?" I asked, walking up to sit beside him.

"I followed you out into the desert, Contessa. I thought maybe you would bring me home. Do you have any idea how long you were gone?" he asked.

"No, I don't. Maybe a couple of hours?"

"Try forty days! You just left me there and I was all alone and then guess who showed up!" He paused and took a breath. "None other than Skinner," he said.

"He did?" I gasped. "How did he get back in here?"

"It doesn't matter. He's gone now."

"What did he say? What did he want?"

"He offered to give me things if I would trade places with him."

"What kinds of things?" I asked, sitting down beside him.

"Not anything that attracted me, that's for sure. I told him to get lost—three times, and finally he did."

"Why do you look so sad then?" I asked.

"Because I have a feeling he will be back."

What Jess did not tell his sister was what he had really said to him. He had said, "Skinner, you can do anything to me you want. I know how you are. But if you touch one hair on my sister's head, or try to diminish her honor in any way, you will never be forgiven. Even I can't help you then."

Jess thought about these words as he watched his sister reaching out to comfort him. He kicked the swing so it would rock some more, and take their minds away.

▪ ▪ ▪

"Jess, come on." I finally said, "Let's go get something to eat," trying to cheer him up.

I offered to make him a honey and pita bread sandwich, his favorite, yet that night and the next, Jess did not emerge from his room.

A few days later he seemed himself again, whistling and singing. It seems the Ranch Hands had gathered around him and let him drive the pickup truck out in the fields.

Jess loves a crowd. Dad looked out at him one day, sitting on his haunches near the corral, laughing with a group of the Ranch Hands, drawing in the dirt with a stick in his hand.

He chuckled. "That boy…whenever two or more workers are gathered together, there you'll find him, right in the midst of them."

Me, however, I prefer talking one-on-one. Mom says it is because I like to go deep in conversation, and explore every angle of a subject, and that takes time. I also love to reflect on things in silence, sometimes for hours or days. Not just anyone can handle that kind of silent communion.

I find that crowds usually get too loud to hear what I am saying, especially since Dad says I speak in a still, small voice much of the time.

▪ ▪ ▪

Chapter Five

I was out grooming Espiritu in the barn, when Jess appeared at the entrance. He stood there a long time, cleared his throat, and then said, "I challenge you both to a race!"

"And what are you going to ride?" I asked. "Your imagination?"

"Oh, I have a noble steed," he assured me. "Mom and Dad gave me a mount, as well." With that he turned and went to the side of the barn, saying, "Come on, now, come on." When he walked back in I fell back on the hay, I was laughing so hard. For what our parents had given him was nothing but a donkey.

"His name is Verdad," Jess said, lifting his shoulders with dignity. He whispered something into one of its huge ears and the donkey nodded its head.

"Brother, I refuse to race you," I laughed. "I won't insult Espiritu like that. I was warned never to quench her spirit, no matter what."

"You just wait and see, Contessa Shekhinah Adonai," Jess said, using my full name. "Verdad and Espiritu will end up at the same place, at the same time. Someday. Mark my words."

Jess was always saying that lately: "Mark my words."

Frankly, I found it annoying. But, as a matter of fact, I did begin to write them down. Those that I could remember.

The Experiment

One day Dad sprinkled rose petals from the porch, leading past the clothesline — out past the studio—past the Library and Lab—right up to the Gate. He asked Mom to follow him there, leading her blindfolded for part of the way. He invited us to follow along with them.

When we got to the Gate he removed the blindfold and said to Mom, "Ta Dah!" Just below us, in a glen by a waterfall, stood two magnificent creations. They seemed just like us —but more dense.... Not quite so iridescent.

The new creations couldn't see us. Dad said he didn't want to alarm them until they adjusted to his scent and their new surroundings.

Dad turned to Mom and said, "Honey, I modeled them after us. That one there looks like me, except with better abs. I know you've been walking by and rubbing my belly, saying I have been spending too much time sitting under the lotus tree..."

"This one," he said, pointing with excitement in his eyes— "is made in the image of you! You were my inspiration."

Mom stood in silence, tears welling in her eyes. We were delighted—amazed—stunned.

"Wow, this sure beats the dinosaurs," I said.

Jess muttered to me under his breath, "Yeah, and this time he got the arms right, too."

Mom looked at Dad and said, "This is *Very* good." "This *Is* very good," he repeated to himself, obviously quite pleased.

Mom said, "Who's going to teach them how to read? I will start a literacy program first thing in the morning."

I started jumping up and down. "I want to show them the Library and the Lab and the Studio!"

Jess said, "I want to take them fishing!"

Dad just chuckled his deepest laugh. "One thing at a time," he smiled. "One thing at a time."

We all turned toward the house. Mom and Dad walked back ahead of us, holding hands.

▪ ▪ ▪

Skinner In the the Garden

After their exile, Skinner and EZ had positioned themselves right by the Gate so they could see what was going on. Ahh yes...the Experiment. Skinner had watched with great interest while Al had sculpted and carved, fashioned and shaped, and then breathed life into...

Skinner felt nauseated as he gazed down on the two Whatevers. They were parading around in their birthday suits just like they owned the place. Apparently, Al considered them "works of art." Skinner thought he had overheard Al calling them names, although Skinner's ears weren't what they used to be. In fact, EZ had said, "I can't see any ears on you at all," one day when they were hanging around. Skinner thought the male was called "A. Dumb" and the female "Heave" or something like that.

"What are you gonna do now, Skinner?" EZ asked.

Skinner flicked his tongue a lot when he thought, and there was a whole lot of flicking going on. Suddenly he said, "I've got an idea."

"Watch this," he whispered as he slithered over to the female Whatever.

"I think you need something to cover up that cellulite," he suggested.

"What's cellulite?" she asked.

"Oh My God. It is the ugliest thing—second only to wrinkles!" Skinner declared. "What are wrinkles?" she asked innocently, suddenly standing up, concerned.

Skinner quickly wrapped himself around her ankle and through selectively applied pressure guided her over to a small pond. There he had her look down at her reflection. As she was staring at herself, he crawled up one side of her body and positioned himself right next to her ear. He knew that if she looked beyond her reflection into the deeper pools of life, like Tess did, then the battle would be lost. He had to act now.

He quickly began to whisper as he sent a jolt down her thigh.

"There is no part of you that doesn't need work. And the parts we can't work on—you must cover up. Here—take these fig leaves." EZ stepped up and handed them to her. "They are not nearly as fat as you are but will have to do until I start a new industry or two. Trust me. I alone will be able to help you feel and stay beautiful." He smiled to himself, knowing that his work was to make sure she would never feel beautiful enough--ever.

Heave looked down at her reflection, with confusion now forming on her face. Skinner realized his job would be to keep her gazing at her looks for as long as possible. Because while she was doing that, he would be so much more free to do other things without her knowledge. Yes, keeping her "at the mirror and out of the studio" was going to be one his major mantras from now on.

"Come on EZ," he said. "Let's go."

"That wasn't hard," muttered EZ as he looked over at the Whatever staring at herself in the pond.

"And give me that extra fig leaf you're hiding," Skinner hissed. "A. Dumb will no doubt be claiming that he needs a bigger one."

▪ ▪ ▪

After that things went down pretty fast. Skinner remembered the details fondly.

Skinner handed the apple he had scanned that night to Heave and she handed it to A. Dumb and he bit into it and said, "Ow, there's something in this apple." Sure enough, he found a rolled up tiny scroll. A. Dumb and Heave had a hard time reading the words since they had skipped their first literacy lesson with Meg, wanting just to make out instead. So Skinner whispered and filled in whenever A. Dumb and Heave stumbled over the characters, which, in fact, was pretty often. He whispered most in A. Dumb's ear since Heave kept distracting herself by leaning down and looking at herself in the pond.

Suddenly, A. Dumb declared out loud, "Heave, I was created first and you were taken from below my armpit!" Skinner could barely contain himself at this interpretation, almost falling out of the tree he was shivering so much with glee. "From now on we don't create together. From now on, you must follow me!" Pop! Skinner's left leg started to emerge.

"In fact, you must obey ME at all times in all things, " A. Dumb continued. "I am the center of your world. Your desire will always be towards me!"

Pop. Pop! In came leg number two. Skinner could sit up now on the tree branch.

A. Dumb sputtered on, ad libbing as he went. "And do not ever try to teach me anything. I will be the one teaching you!"

(There! That will put Meg in her place, Skinner thought... Meg, that Know-it-all, Be-it-all, Beginning-of-all, End-of-all. Ha! Skinner had learned one lesson from her, and that was this—begin

with the end in mind. How fortunate he was to be here now, in the Garden, in this phase of the Experiment.)

Skinner and EZ quickly began chanting from the shadows, "You da Man! You da Man!" as A. Dumb began to march around. Skinner had learned a thing or two from observing the Greek chorus down the road. Currently, their act hadn't made it to the Ranch, yet he liked their emphasis on all male voices speaking from the shadows. It was a powerful tool indeed.

With each sentence A. Dumb spoke about separation and superiority, Skinner's hands and then his fingers began to fill in, one by one.

When A. Dumb finally declared, "I am the Boss of everything here—every creature, every mountain was made just for me! And you too, Heave, you were made just for me, and to have my children, and bear them in pain!" Pop! Pop! Pop! Skinner snapped back up on his feet again—fully formed, and able to stand erect, as it were.

("Wow, I think I like this guy," Skinner thought. "Maybe he's got potential.")

Just then, Al walked back into the garden. "What is going on here?" he asked. "Why is she hiding her face from me? Is that a bruise under her eye?"

"It's all her fault," cried A. Dumb. "She made me lose my temper. Something just came over me, and I hit her."

Suddenly Al roared like Skinner had never heard him roar before.

There was a lot of crying and denying. Mike and Gabriel showed up with torches again. Somebody had to leave. The Gate was locked. Blah Blah Blah.

But the important thing now was that Skinner was back on his feet— able to walk among them like the mighty one he was— and had been—before...well...you know.

Heave looked down where Skinner had been, but he was already gone, leaving behind a little trail of dust.

"Wow, Skinner can move so much faster since these two Whatevers came along," EZ thought as he struggled to keep up with him. "Is it my imagination or are his legs even longer now than they were on the Ranch?"

▪ ▪ ▪

Chapter Seven

The next day, Dad came home in a fury. His usually tanned face had turned almost pale with rage. He slammed the door on the front porch so hard a photograph that had hung over the door fell down and shattered. I went over to pick it up and noticed it was of a photo of the two Creations. The glass had shattered so badly it was hard to recognize their faces. I carefully put it back up high on the shelf as Dad went into the mudroom with Mom.

We have now learned that the original intent of Dad's experiment was to have the Creations live with us right here on the Ranch. But something has gone terribly wrong. I'm sure Skinner has something to do with it.

The Triple A has been tasked with creating a new sustainable place for them to live. It is what we now call the Valley Land, which is close but also far away. Dad doesn't go down by the Gate much anymore. I think he needs time to heal.

Creativity is our nature, and it didn't take long for it to spring back into Dad. I walked in one night to find Mom and Dad comparing notes from their day's work. It is amazing to me how often they end up working on parallel designs.

Mom, for example, came up with a design for a sea creature that has a translucent rounded head, with long dangling threads.

Dad, meanwhile, came up with a design for a galaxy activity called a nebula, which is really a star changing form. When he demonstrated the design for the nebula on the five-dimensional studio screen, Mom laughed that his design looked like her "jelly fish," except with more colors.

One day Jess and I were messing around drawing chalk ideas on some flat stones outside the barn. Jess drew a horse with a really long neck and I filled it in with polka dots. Jess then drew a skinny tail and I put two little bumps on its head. The very next day we looked out and there that very creature was staring right back at us through the second-story window. Mom smiled. "I'm calling this one a giraffe. Great design work, you two." Oh how we loved the way she would surprise us—taking our doodles and drawings and making them come alive.

With plants and in most of nature they agreed to use mathematical formulas to keep everything looking good in proportion.

The formula is 1 to .618, often rounded up to 1 to point 7. This proportion, called the Golden Mean, is demonstrated even in Valley Landers, whose heads are one seventh of their whole bodies. Mom handed this formula off to the Triple A team. They played around with it in leaves, trees, flowers, animals, you name it. If it has a pleasing proportion, the Golden Mean is probably in there somewhere.

Yesterday we got a surprise package at the Gate. It was wrapped in banana leaves, and signed, "From Your friend, Maya." Chattanango opened it up, him being Security and all, and found a lovely, dark brown concoction that melted in his hands. He took a sniff, tasted it, and wow did his eyes light up. He rushed some over to Mom and Dad, who also took a lick. And another. And another. Next thing I know Mom grabs a bottle of wine, takes Dad by the hand, and says, "We will see you all later." And this was right in the middle of the day!

I have nicknamed the gift CoCoLoco, because everyone is so crazy about it now. Dad got the idea to mix some in with his coffee, and now the Ranch Hands are lining up at the kitchen, wanting him to make more. Mom joked he could open up a stand and start just making this stuff full time. He laughed, "We'd have to put one on every corner of the Ranch, and then how would any work get done?" Mom is always coming up with ideas.

She loves connecting dots and seeing how one activity could be valuable for a particular group if it were refined this way or that. Sometimes, she hardly goes to bed at night, making sure everyone is working on her ideas. Dad calls out to her, "Honey, it's time for bed," and she yells back, "Be right there!" But then she works three or four more hours, writing out thank-you notes and job well done cards to the workers.

▪ ▪ ▪

Chapter Eight

It isn't all work at the Ranch. Sure, there is plenty to do, with the gardening, designing, laundry, separating the sheep from the goats, the wheat from the chaff, and all that. But on the sixth day, every week, Dad says, "Enough of working. It is time for golf."

Q has been assigned to be his caddy. Mom thinks this will help Q pay attention to details and learn to discern light from dark. She said, "Believe me, from what I have seen of the score keeping, shades of gray are part of every golf game."

One time, Q made the mistake of taking a message from a Ranch Hand at the Gate. Dad looked down at the note that was handed to him and said, "King? They want a king now? I am supposed to be their king!" He threw the paper down and seemed perplexed the rest of the game. He wrote down, "Now I shall send you Prophets," and that message was sent back to them. I'm sure it was something the Valley Landers were up to, as they have become high maintenance, shall we say.

But most of the time, when playing golf, Dad is relaxed. Dad lines up at the tee, and Q lays down a comet, Dad's favorite golf ball. They aren't much to look at when you set them on the tee, but when he whacks them, wow! We all "oooh" and "ahhh."

On the holes that are closer in, Dad turns and asks Q, "Which club should I use?" Q made the big mistake once of saying, "The One Iron." Jess whispered, "I've heard that not even Dad can hit with a one iron." Sure enough, when Dad hit the comet, it flew wildly off course. Unfortunately, it ended up in the Black Hole, and when Q reached in to try to retrieve it he almost disappeared.

He kept yelling, "Grab my feet! Grab my feet!" Chattanango was finally able to pull him out of it. Q didn't say much for the next few days, and someone, I don't know who, wrapped the one iron around a tree.

There are so many golf balls out there, they even look like patterns. I learned later that Valley Landers called them constellations and gave them names.

But every golf game ends the same way—at the 19th hole. Chattanango and crew prepare a barbecue. Often this coincides with an event from the Valley Land.

One particular day I remember, we were sitting around the table, munching the last of our corn on the cob, when Chattanango walked up, smelling like fire.

"What is it, Nango?" asked Mom as she scooped out more potato salad.

"Elijah just arrived with his chariot. Let me tell you, his horses were wild! It took all the power I had just to calm them down enough to get into their stalls."

Dad threw his head back and laughed. "I knew when I threw another burger on the fire, Elijah would show up. He likes his meat burnt to a crisp. Here Tess, go give him this, will you?"

And that is how I ended up taking a plate of food to Elijah. He was sort of hard to talk to. For one thing, he kept looking for his cloak, saying he must have left it with Elisha. Then, he kept looking over his shoulder for someone named Jezebel. He was so afraid we were going to run out of oil that he kept bringing jugs in and setting them side by side. When he tried to throw himself over a napping Jess, Dad finally had to take him aside and say, "Elijah, you need some rest. Why don't you go out to the wilderness for a while? Change your diet....eat some protein and honey."

With that Elijah headed off, nodding in recognition to a still-startled Jess as he went away.

▪ ▪ ▪

Breakfast at the Ranch is always the same. Jess and I have blueberries and oatmeal. We crack each other up, making faces with two blueberry eyes in the oatmeal, with a slice of apple for a nose, or a peach for a smile.

Mom gets into the game, drawing faces in the swirls of cream in her morning coffee. She does this with the clouds, too, and sometimes we try to recognize animals in them.

Dad takes over the stove, cooking up his usual poached egg. He had to rename it "free range egg," however, since Mom hates the word "poached." Yesterday when Jess and I were putting away the silverware, Jess took a spoon and started drumming it on the table. I picked up a bigger one and started pounding out a beat to match it. Mom walked in and stood there a minute, just listening. We got louder and louder and more creative, adding "Chick a chicka boom/Waow Waow" vocal rhythms. "You two need to take this show down the road!" she exclaimed. "The further, the better," Dad added, smiling and shaking his head.

Mom and I have started to take afternoon hikes along the river. She will be walking along and then she will reach down and pick up a rock for me to look at, and ask, "What do you see?" First, I just said simply, "A rock." This brought a frown to her face. "Contessa, we didn't raise you just to see the obvious." I tried harder, seeing suddenly "A fish." And "a star." Then she would turn it upside down and ask, "What else do you see?" I would have to look more closely to please her, and only then would I notice the flower, or the owl's eye, in the very same rock. The more patterns I recognize, the more praise I get.

Meanwhile, Dad has started walking with Jess among the lilies in the field.

I was lying on the bed one night, watching Mom prepare for her date night with Dad.

"What does the word 'blaspheme' mean?" I asked her, with my pencil poised over my notebook in order to record her answer.

"Well, it means revile or abuse, but the root word really means 'to blame.' she replied, putting her earrings on. "Why do you ask?"

"This is one of the words Jess was studying at the Library the other day." I paused. "I hope I never have to hear it used," I said, with some finality.

"I hope you don't either," said Mom, now fully dressed and ready to go downstairs. She leaned over and gave me a kiss and said, "You and your brother behave!" "Don't we always?" I asked. "Where are you and Dad going tonight?"

"Your father said it was going to be a surprise—something about a new place called The Rabbit Hole."

▪ ▪ ▪

Last week Mom took me in for a formal meeting with Algo Rithm, the head of the Triple A. "She's yours in the afternoons now," she said. Algo is going to personally mentor me in solving complex problems in a very methodical step by step process, with an advanced specialization in Pattern Recognition.

One project I've been thinking about is how to develop an automatic timer so Shalomar doesn't have to physically stand at the controls and manually raise and set the sun each day. And wouldn't it be nice if the seasons could pretty much come at the same time, instead of whenever Shalomar feels like it? I talked to Algo and the team about each of these ideas. They smiled and said, "Sketch it out, study it, test it, improve on it, and we will help you make it happen."

Sometimes Q comes to visit me in the Lab. "Hi Q," I say to him while I am working away. "The new name is Nike," he said one day, showing me his new black jersey with a big check mark on it. "Just do it do it do it!" he rapped as he got closer. I looked at him suspiciously, and then said, "Q, you know we don't accept endorsement deals up here. Especially from the Greeks. Go take that back to the Gate!" I said sharply, concerned that he had violated a known rule. Then, when I remembered what he was trying to accomplish, I said in a softer tone, "You can make it into the Triple A on your own power. You don't need to use someone else's label to get you there." He eventually agreed and flew half-heartedly out the door.

▪ ▪ ▪

Some of the projects going on in the Lab are very serious ones indeed. For example, I know that they are all working feverishly on creating a universal thermal control system, especially since Skinner ravaged Tierra. There are places in her heart now where nothing grows, and no living thing can survive. Her eyelashes are starting to fall out, one by one. Mom goes out and sits with her sometimes, and says she's ready to listen whenever Tierra is ready to talk. Dad keeps checking on her, asking, "Is everything OK, Darling? Is there anything I can bring you?" I am not sure what I can do to help. Jess says he thinks her healing is going to take some time.

▪ ▪ ▪

Chapter Nine

I love to study. Mom likes to design. Jess likes to do whatever Dad tells him to do, and Dad loves to go into his media room and people watch. He settles into his arm chair and catches up on the Valley Lander activities.

We walk by and hear him cheering, "Way to go!" Or I hear him moan, "Not again." Occasionally we dare to look in at the score. One time after hearing him cheer, we looked in and saw: David: 1. Goliath: 0. Another time, I looked in and saw "Ninevah: -10. Jonah: 0." That contest became a real close one, with Ninevah finally turning the score around just before the buzzer went off. Jonah wasn't too happy, however, about the outcome and he almost quit the team.

One contest that was the first one recorded was between a Valley Lander named Job and Skinner. Somehow, Skinner had managed to place a bet with Dad that Job would turn against Dad when things weren't going so well for him, and Dad said, "You're on." I am glad that one turned out all right, although the show went on way too long for my taste. When Job's friends would come on again and start saying really dumb things, I would want to change the channel. Of course, there were no other channels.

Dad could watch talking heads for hours, but Mom only wants to see something happen. She says, "If they're not going to do anything but talk, what's the point? I'd like to see some action." I agree with her completely, which is why I run outside to play a lot, and she goes to the studio.

But first, to the incident.

Reports had come in from the WECU station in the Valley that the Valley Landers had really gotten things messed up. I mean, they had been bad before, but now they were getting worse. They refused to take the two tablets Dad had sent them through Moses, and they had also become so mean, they were beginning to sacrifice their own children. Mom said they certainly had a rude way of greeting strangers.

Dad decided he couldn't take it anymore. He declared he was going to flood the Valley and be done with the whole Experiment once and for all. He met with the Triple A design team, and of course Mom, who persuaded him to keep at least one family alive, and at least two of every animal. The Triple A worked feverishly getting the right dimensions for a boat that could hold them all. But who could Dad trust to build it? Finally a scout came back and said, "I know someone." And that is how Noah was chosen.

Noah worked hard and got everything ready. Then Dad walked up to the weather station and very reluctantly but deliberately turned on the spigots. Shalomar had to step aside, as this was Dad's project through and through.

For forty days and forty nights, Dad stood at the controls. Finally, one of the doves I had designed was sent out to look for land.

She came back bearing an olive branch and Dad then said, "That is enough. What is done is done." He was exhausted. He hadn't slept a wink. But before he turned to go Mom said,

"Honey, wouldn't it be nice if you promised never to do this again?" She didn't want the Valley Landers to always be afraid of Dad. There was no point in that.

He said, "You're right." Then she turned to me and said, "Tess, why don't you come up with a symbol real quick?"

"Really? You want me to design it?" I was ecstatic. What could symbolize a promise? I thought to myself. Maybe a circle. I ran into the studio, looking desperately for the color I wanted. Which color would work best? Blue? Yes. The blue of the sky. The blue of Crystal Lake.

But wait. What about red? The red of the rose or yellow, like the sunflower. Or what about magenta, the color of midnight. Of course Chattanango's favorite color, indigo, had to be included. I couldn't pick just one so I grabbed a handful of all the colors and ran back up to the weather station. Dad looked down at my choices, and for the first time in forty days he smiled. So, that's what I drew in the sky. Dad's big smile. From the Ranch it is a complete circle, while I understand in the Valley they can only see half of it.

▪ ▪ ▪

After that Dad and Mom put Jess and I in charge of a new program they had initiated called "The Prophet-Making Tours." We would go down to the Gate and meet some Valley Landers who had been handpicked, and greet them, check their tickets, and then seat them on the bus. We weren't supposed to show them everything, but just parts of the Ranch, so they could go back and describe to the Valley what things could be like if they behaved. Jess checked off their names while I checked their tickets. "Isaiah." Check. "Jeremiah." Check. "Ezekiel." Check. And so on. Then Jess would describe different things Dad wanted them to see. "Over here, you will notice the lions laying down with the lambs." Or I might say, "Notice how everyone gets along here, and all the Ranch Hands get to sit under their own fig tree."

Then we would file in to the dining hall and be greeted by the Ranch Hands, who were careful to sit in their assigned places. Mom was especially adamant about this. She said it created order.

Cleanliness would sit next to Godliness, of course. Then Amor, Alegría, Paz, Paciencia, and Bondad gathered on one side of the table. Generosidad, Fidelidad, Suavidad, and Mí Control filled in the remaining seats. Chattanango, Q, Shalomar, and the Triple A all worked on shifts, so they would file in and greet people as long as there was coverage.

One time Dad, after hearing from some of the Judges he sent down, took the prophets on a midnight tour, showing them the incinerator and the Badlands, and getting them prepared for the worst. I didn't know about this until I started reading some of the reports that came back later.

I asked Dad and Mom how Valley Landers could be so cruel to one another, and they said, "They have been given the power of free will. They get to choose how they act and what they believe."

"Why would anyone choose to be cut off from The Ranch like that, and create such images of horror? Why do they choose to live alone, struggling along, when they could have so much fun being with us?" I wondered.

"It would have been easier if your father hadn't given them free will," Mom continued. "But he wanted it that way, saying, 'How else will we know that they love us, just for us?'"

■ ■ ■

Chapter Ten

We were all in shock when even the Judges Dad had appointed couldn't get the Valley Landers to behave. Instead, they just kept getting further and further away from us in their thoughts and actions.

One day, Dad had a conference call with the Judges and Prophets. They told him that the Valley Lander shepherds were not tending and caring for the sheep, like they were supposed to, but instead were caring only for themselves. This made Dad very angry. He wrote out a full memo on his feelings and sent it back with the prophet Ezekiel. Here is some of what he wrote:

MEMO to Shepherds

You have not taken care of the weak. You have not tended the sick or bound up the injured. You have not gone looking for those who have wandered away and are lost. Instead, you have ruled them with harshness and cruelty. They have wandered through all the mountains and all the hills, across the face of the earth, yet no one has gone to search for them.

(Ezekiel 34: 4 New Living Translation)

The more he thought about it, the angrier he got. He has not been very happy lately at all.

▪ ▪ ▪

Jess and I went for a long walk the next day, talking about the Prophet's Tour and the Judges report. We were trying to figure out why Valley Landers could be so careless with the treasures entrusted to them, and why they wouldn't seek Dad and Mom's guidance on matters large and small. "Skinner is down there stirring things up, and for whatever reason, he is able to get others to go along with him," I said sadly. "It has to stop," Jess said quietly, shaking his head. "It simply has to stop." I asked him, "Do you think you have to scare someone into acting in their own best interest?" Mom had voiced something similar the night before. Jess thought for a long time and then said, "I think there is a better way." Tonight we are sad because we realize that not even the flood, the rainbow promise, or the prophets have been enough to turn things around.

▪ ▪ ▪

Chapter Eleven

On the last day of the tour Dad said, "I am going to be busy this morning comforting Jeremiah. It seems he can't stop weeping. Daniel, you and your friends will go with Contessa to see the lions. I think Skinner fed them before he left, but just want you to make sure."

Mom got into the golf cart with Isaiah, saying she was going to run him by Reunion Hall and show him what it looks like when those who went forth weeping, carrying their tears, come back singing, carrying their sheaves. Before they left she asked, "Jess, could you please take Ezekiel and show him the river?"

Jess said he would be glad to, but he was supposed to go to the studio and work on timelines with Elijah.

Then Chattanango volunteered, saying, "I will take him. That way nobody will fall in." He stopped by the tool shed and got out the cubit measuring stick before he left. He told me later he walked Ezekiel over the hill and down towards the place where the stream becomes a river and flows into the sea. He showed him the workers on either side of the stream, happily fishing all day. He showed him the many different kinds of fish swimming in the river. He had him taste one of the fruits growing on the tree branches, telling him it would not only feed him, but make him feel better when he got to the Valley. He showed him all these things, and Ezekiel promised him he would remember it with the numbers 4 and 7 (a memory device he used).

We finished off the tour by taking them all over to the new development, where Dad was preparing to build the many mansions Jess and the Triple A were designing.

There had been some environmental concerns from the Triple A when they learned they might be building on a valley of old bones, but Mom said, "When I breathe on them, they shall rise up, a great and exceeding army." As Ezekiel watched in amazement, that is exactly what happened, and then we had the problem of an exceeding great army standing around.

(I think Dad ended up putting them on a bus to Jericho.)

Finally, the tour was complete. The Prophets thanked us for our work with them and then got on the bus to go over to the Gate, where they then stepped into the chariot Elijah had brought over for that very purpose. As they were thundering off, I heard Jonah lean over to Ezekiel and shout, "Now, exactly how big was that fish you saw?"

We always felt better after a Prophet's tour was over, thinking surely they could get the message to the Valley Landers, and we could go about our time peacefully on the Ranch, without constant interruptions from them.

Yet, even their best efforts did not work. Dad sat down with Mom one night at the kitchen table with a long list he had drawn out on a yellow tablet. On one side, he had written down all the good things the Valley Landers had done. On the other side, he had written all the bad things they had done. The bad list was longer, to be sure.

He said, "I built them a Garden. They messed that up. We blessed them with children, and one of them killed the other one. I finally find a good man, Abraham, willing to relocate, and he ends up with sons who can't get along. They have children who act out, and I decide that maybe some time making bricks will teach them a lesson."

"Honey, don't forget Moses," Mom said, putting a big star by his name. "He has always been a good friend to you."

"That's true," Dad said, circling his name.

"And Joshua, he is a great leader, afraid of nothing," Mom said, trying to even up the good list with the bad.

"Nehemiah, what a great contractor," Dad nodded, adding to her positive list, and so on.

Their conversation lasted long into the night. I had crawled down to listen to it, laying my head down on my arms right behind the stairs. Jess heard me get up, and he tiptoed down right behind me and sat on the very bottom step, with barely his toes showing past the wall.

"Tuck them in!" I whispered.

"I can't!" he whispered back. "Toes don't retract!"

They were so engrossed in their conversation, however, that they didn't even notice us. Dad continued, "Well, maybe this David will be a man after my own heart. He certainly has the potential."

"I know," said Mom, agreeing. "And can you believe that Jonathan gave up his throne for him?" I wanted to stay awake and hear the rest, but I guess Jess and I fell asleep. I think Chattanango found us and carried us up the stairs.

■ ■ ■

Chapter Twelve

Mom and Dad talked late into the night. We could hear them murmuring through the walls. Something in their tone seemed off. It was not the usual happy sounds that emanated from their conversations. The next morning, Dad and Jess went off together very early and did not return until late afternoon. They didn't even take their fishing poles, so I knew something was up.

We were just sitting down to supper, and Jess asked for the honey to be passed. Dad said, "I have an announcement to make. Things are going to change around here. Tess, you are to stay here on the Ranch and continue your studies. Jess is going to have to leave the Ranch." I gasped when I heard that, but he continued. "We've placed him with a very nice family in the Valley. He has some very important work to do."

I glanced at Jess, and then at Dad. Mom had her head down and was silently stirring her food. Jess, never one to question why, asked simply, "When do I leave?"

"Soon, Son. Very soon." We finished the meal in silence. I was barely able to swallow my food. Nobody slept well that night, especially me. What did Dad mean that Jess had to leave?

▪ ▪ ▪

Ever since he learned he is going away, Jess doesn't joke around as much as he used to. After all our chores are done I'll say, "Jess, you must be very tired. Come and sit with me for a while." I will have packed us a picnic of his favorite things, and we'll go sit on the pier. We don't say much, just sit there and listen to the crickets and watch the fireflies start to spark up the twilight. Fireflies always make him smile. As I sit there looking at him, I realize his smile is far too precious to ever have it fade.

I keep wondering if there is anything I can do so he doesn't have to leave.

Jess gets up early every morning now to walk with Mom out to the well. She likes to draw water from this special well for her painting, saying it produces living art. Sometimes she leans against the well and he sits on the ground facing her, and they just talk.

I think she is also showing him how to change the properties of water, saying this will come in handy for him later on. He told me he is only supposed to do this on very special occasions, however, and never just to show off.

Sometimes now when we are just hanging out, reading in the loft at the barn, a serious look will come over him and I will ask, "Jess, what's wrong?" "Oh, it's nothing, Sis," he says, "nothing I can't handle." And then he reaches over and messes up my hair. He knows how much I hate to have my hair messed up.

▪ ▪ ▪

That next morning, Mom and I went to the studio, gathering up yarn for the weavers to work with that day. Neither one of us said anything. Time suddenly seemed to move so slowly—something I had never experienced before on the Ranch.

Later that afternoon, we heard boots scraping on the porch, and then Dad and Jess walked in to the living room together. Dad looked at over at us and said, “It’s time.” He turned to Jess and said, “Get your things together, Son. Gabe is taking you down tomorrow. “

Jess nodded, went over and hugged Mom, and then asked to be excused. I fell in silently beside him as he started walking, knowing where we would be going. When we got there we walked out to the end of the pier and sat down, taking off our boots and socks. We dangled our feet over the water just as the sun was starting to go down.

“I don’t want to leave you, Tess,” he said. “I don’t want to leave any of this.”

“I know, Jess,” I said, putting my arm around him.

“Promise me one thing, will you?” he asked, looking straight ahead. “Promise me that if I call for you, you will come to me, no matter what.”

“I promise, Jess. I will.”

As he dipped his toe in the water, I noticed that the lake suddenly turned blood red.

We sat like that for a long time, not wanting to get up and face what the next day would bring. Finally, Chattanango walked up behind us and touched us on the shoulder, saying softly, “Come on now, kids, it’s time to go.” And even though we felt almost grown up now, we each put our hands in his like two little children as we walked back to the house.

■ ■ ■

That night Mom prepared a banquet, saying, "Tonight is a special night. Dad has asked all the Ranch Hands to join us."

One by one they came in, even Shalomar. When I looked up at her quizzically she said, "It's ok. I set the controls to eclipse. I can be here for a little while." Once everybody had a seat, Dad raised his glass and said, "Jess, tonight you are old enough to have your first taste of this." Jess reached for the cup expectantly and his eyes grew wide as he sipped the wine.

"Tonight, my darling bride, my loving daughter, and my beloved son, this will be our last supper together for a while…" Dad choked up and couldn't continue, leaning his head down almost like he was going to fall.

Jess quickly stood up, put his arm around him, and said, "I will always remember this—remember each of you," nodding slowly to each of us. Then he raised his glass and said, "From now on, whenever you drink wine together please remember me."

▪ ▪ ▪

The next morning we were up before dawn. Gabe was at the wheel of the truck, staring straight ahead. Mike had loaded up everything that what was needed, including Verdad, who was tied up in a trailer behind the truck with his big ears sticking out.

"Here, I wanted to give you this," I said, walking up to Jess. "I made it myself." He looked down at the smooth polished stone, which I had carved in the shape of a dove. "Is that a bird, or a rocking chair?" he joked, poking me in the ribs. He started to speak, but then something caught in his throat. He coughed a minute and then said, "I love it." He put the dove in his pocket, turned away, and wiped something from his eyes.

"I've got something for you, too," Jess said. He slowly removed the leather pouch he wore around his neck all the time. He kept it for collecting rocks he liked or feathers from birds that had fallen to the ground. I looked inside and couldn't see anything at first. I put the pouch around my neck and turned towards him again. He hugged Dad and Mom and all the Ranch Hands. Then he got into the truck, closed the door, and rolled down the window. He reached out and took my hand, saying:

"Remember your promise!"

"I will," I said, holding onto his hand even as the truck began to pull away.

I began walking and then running alongside it, until finally, I couldn't keep up anymore. I just stood there choking back tears as my brother disappeared down the road.

That night I took off the pouch, opened it and turned it upside down, looking for what he had given me. At first I couldn't see anything, but finally, there on the fluffy white comforter I found it.

It was a mustard seed.

▪ ▪ ▪

Fia's neck was aching and her eyes welled with tears in the cave as she continued reading the diary. She thought about Tess having to say goodbye to Jess. She knew all too well the hole in a family created when a loved one was suddenly gone—was no longer showing up at the breakfast table. She couldn't help but remember Nissi shouting "See ya!" as he walked out the door, grabbing his backpack with one hand and a piece of toast off her plate with the other. Fia wondered how Tess would get by without her brother. They had been inseparable it seemed, just like she and Nissi had been.

Fia continued reading, as one of her tears fell onto the page.

▪ ▪ ▪

Chapter Thirteen

It seemed like the sun didn't rise or set the next day, or the next. Nothing was the same without him. I had little energy and almost no appetite. Mom finally came into my room and said, "Come on, Tessa my love, get up. I want to show you something. Get your hat and your backpack. This hike is going to take awhile."

Mom and I began hiking up the trail that led into the forest. We passed the meadow and crossed the stream and then began climbing a steeper hill that had many switchbacks. At one point, I almost stumbled, and I could hear a rock go tumbling down, way down into the canyon below us. "Careful, Tessa, this way is hard, and few have ever found it." Finally, we rounded a bend, and I saw it. A waterfall, unlike anything I had ever seen. "I've named it Bridal Falls, because it looks like a wedding veil," she said. "This is my secret place, and now I'm showing it to you. We stood there looking at it silently for a long, long time.

Finally she said, "You can stay here as long as you like," patting my knee as she rose to go. Just before she stepped away she said softly, "I miss him too."

I stood there for a moment, trembling, and then stepped under the shimmering cascade.

▪ ▪ ▪

I don't know what I would have done without Chattanango. He drew closer to me, knowing how lonely I was without Jess. Dad and Mom seemed even busier than before, so often it was Chattanango and me, taking walks in the evening or going out to watch the fireflies.

Chattanango's job is hard to describe. Mom says he was one of the first to hold me when I was "poured forth." I remember him rocking me to sleep when Mom was busy in the studio. He used to take my little hands in his and carefully clean under my fingernails. "I know you've been digging in the dirt, little girl, just like your mother does. But that is no way for a lady to show up at the dinner table."

Dad had him teach me some wrestling moves, saying Mom wanted me to be very strong. "This is the one I used on that Valley Lander Jacob," Chattanango said, sweeping me off my feet. "He limped the rest of his life after that battle!"

"Now why would you say that like it was a good thing?" I asked, reaching up to him and smiling. As he reached down to help me up I quickly grabbed his wrist with both hands, planted my feet on his washboard abs, and flipped him over me. He landed with a thud. He lay there silently for a moment, stunned at what had happened.

"I give up! I am no match for you, Contessa," he said, laughing while trying to catch his breath. Mom, who was watching on the sidelines, laughed. "Well done, both of you! Now let's go get some fresh fruit and vegetables!" (She considers this a reward.)

As we walked off I heard Chattanango say to Dad, "Contessa is really strong!"

"Don't I know it," Dad chuckled. "You're lucky she didn't use the Bat move on you."

"What's that?" he asked, dusting himself off.

"She gazes right at you, bats those eyelashes slowly three times, and the next thing you know your whole being is wrapped around her little finger."

▪ ▪ ▪

This is the copy of the birth announcement Dad and Mom sent out after I was born. Chattanango keeps a copy of it with him in his messenger bag, sometimes just to read to me. He began to read it to me every day, especially when I was missing Jess.

Here it is, in its entirety. (It's really long. Mom said when I was born Dad just went on and on about me. I think this list is proof positive that she wasn't exaggerating.)

Al and Meg are pleased to announce the birth of Contessa Shekhinah Adonai.

"Within her is a spirit intelligent, holy, unique, manifold, subtle, active, incisive, unsullied, lucid, invulnerable, benevolent, shrewd, irresistible, beneficent, friendly to all, steadfast, dependable, unperturbed, almighty, all-surveying, penetrating all intelligent, pure and most subtle spirits. She is quicker to move than any motion. She is so pure, she pervades and permeates all things. She is the breath of the power of God, pure emanation of the glory of the almighty, so nothing impure can find its way into her.

She is a reflection of the eternal light, untarnished mirror of God's active power, and image of all goodness.

Although alone, she can do all. Herself unchanging, she makes all things new. She turns people into God's friends and prophets.

She is indeed more splendid than the sun, and outshines all the constellations.

She deploys her strength from one end of the world to the other, and she governs the whole world for its good." (Book of Wisdom, 7:22-30. Jerusalem Bible.)

Sometimes Mom would brush my hair and have me read these words out loud while she groomed me. "This is who you are, Contessa. Who you were created to be."

▪ ▪ ▪

One day Mom called me into her studio. She said, "Tess, here is your assignment. I want you to go by yourself into the forest, and come back at the end of the day and tell me all about it." So, I eagerly took off, singing at the top of my lungs as I went. I picked up a stick and used it to smack some of the tree trunks while I walked along. I called out to the birds and squirrels. I tried to imitate the little chucking sounds they made. Finally, I picked a handful of the prettiest flowers I could find, yanking them out by their roots in my hurry. I came running back in the house, flowers in hand, and told Mom exactly all the things I had done in the forest.

She sat for a few moments, and then said "Tessa, it sounds like the forest experienced YOU, but you did not experience the forest." I put my head down, disappointed in myself. She said, "Tomorrow, I want you to try again, but this time get very still and listen." So the next day I went out with a far different attitude. I walked quietly along, trying not to disturb its beauty. I found a meadow and lay down on my back, closed my eyes, and just listened. After a few moments I heard it.

There was a symphony of sounds. Bird songs and squirrels chucking to one another. Leaves rustled in the air. Crickets chirped. And then I actually heard the sound of the land itself humming. It was so resonant and so beautiful, I felt I could stay there forever. When I finally did arise and return to Mom I told her simply, "Sounds. So many sounds. All in a symphony."

She smiled and said, "Well done, Contessa. You've completed the lesson. Wisdom always listens before making its own sound."

▪ ▪ ▪

The day after that, I got a big surprise. Dad had me come out to Crystal Lake with him. We walked out on the pier and then he said, "Look down. What do you see?"

Jess was standing knee deep in water in a river and he just looked up and saw me. Dad was there too and he called out, "I am well pleased with you, Son!" John the Baptist, who looked like Elijah, was standing a few feet away. I started to say something and then the Valley sky closed up again.

I'm so glad I gave Jess the dove before he left. I hope it is helping him now. I hope he is holding it close to his heart as he walks through the Valley.

▪ ▪ ▪

Chapter Fourteen

I guess now is as good a time as any to write about what has been foremost on my mind. It all began when I felt the familiar presence at my door.

"What is it, Chattanango?

"This letter was left for you at the Gate."

I took it in my hands and began to read.

"Dear Contessa,

Please forgive me for being so bold. I have spoken to your father about you, and he said we could begin our correspondence. I have heard so much about you from my father, as well as others who have come before him. I am but a man born of woman, but would you do me the honor of meeting me at the Gate? Early or late doesn't matter. I want your beauty more than life itself. Signed simply, S."

Who is "S?" I asked. "He is a Valley Lander is all I know," said Chattanango. "Perhaps you should ask your father."

So I went and found Dad sitting in his private study. Sometimes he would be watching WECU, the channel always tuned to the Valley Land, on a set that hung above the fireplace.

But today he was taking down one record album at a time from his media shelves and lovingly running his fingers over the grooves. When he did so a form would emerge and hover, and then turn into sounds. We knew all of Dad's favorites by name. "The Trumpets of Jericho." "The Laughter of Isaac." "Moses and the Parting of the Seas." "Joseph and the Many-Colored Coat." "Esther at the Banquet Hall."

"What are you listening to, Dad?" I asked. "The Song of Deborah," he replied. "It is full of such passion!"

I asked Dad who "S" was he said, "Oh, that must be Solomon. He is the son of David and he is slated to be king of the Valley Landers soon. He is quite a fellow, that one. I came to him in a dream and asked him what he wanted, now that he was about to rule the world, and do you know what he asked for?" Dad paused and turned to me. "What?" I replied.

"He said he wanted you to be his bride." And because he sees your true worth," said Dad, standing up from his chair, "I plan to give him everything."

And so began what I have to say is the Love Song of my Life. What is it about Solomon that captivated me so? Any words I might write down here would only be an attempt to capture our attraction. I would have to say for me, it was a combination of several factors.

One is that he makes me feel beautiful. He doesn't just say things like, "You look hot!" (Skinner's favorite come-on line).

He goes into detail about how my eyes look, how my neck looks, how my scent drives him to distraction. For a man to take that much time to describe me, comparing me to all the beautiful things I love (lambs, doves, gazelles, lilies, jasmine) means he really takes the time to think about me. He must have asked around to find out what I like, since I never told him. It is like he is getting a Ph.D. in me.

Two is the way he writes to me—little love notes all the time, that he slips under the Gate. Like this one I got three days ago:

"Come my love, my lovely one come… for the winter is past, and the rains are over and gone. Flowers are appearing on the earth…"

This one I got this morning. "How beautiful you are my love, how beautiful you are. There is no flaw in you."

Sometimes he sounds desperate: "Show me your face! Let me hear your voice!"

Or romantic:

"You ravish my heart, my sister, my bride, with a single one of your glances." I love that word "ravish." It sounds like my love will be a feast for him, and that he is famished to be with me.

I love knowing that he is hungry to hear me. Look at this one:

"My dove, hiding in the clefts of the rock, in the coverts of the cliff, cause me to hear your voice!"

His ability to write songs and poetry about me is of course very endearing, as well as the fact that he loves to reflect on things, like I do… Did I say he is really smart?

I also love his hair. It is jet black and shiny—with just a few brown highlights from the sun. It falls down just to his shoulders. (Jess doesn't wear his hair that long. He says when he carries lambs on his shoulders they start nibbling on it, so he keeps it shorter).

Of course, Solomon isn't a shepherd, he is a king, and a poet, and an author, and a builder, and I could go on and on. He stirs feelings in me I didn't know I could have.

When I first saw him coming up the path, after running so hard, I couldn't help but notice the sheen of sweat on his arms. He was wearing a sleeveless tank top, and the little drops of sweat gathering and trickling down his arms was somehow very exciting to me. I looked at the muscles in his arms, and I couldn't even imagine what it would be like to have those magnificent arms embracing me, his fingers softly toying with my hair, which he says "falls down my neck like water."

Perhaps most inexplicably, it is his scent that enchants me.

It is a combination of musk and jasmine, mint and aloe. I know perfume is expensive and treasured in the Valley, and the fact that he uses it lavishly on himself when he comes to see me, well, it works.

He doesn't have to work in the fields, like most Valley Landers, so I guess he gets his upper body strength from the chariot races he participates in all the time.

Yesterday, he told me that he just wants us to run away. I have to admit I am ready to do that. I don't know how much longer I can keep just thinking about him, and not really touching him. If only there was some way I could even bring him to the Ranch….even sneak him into my mother's studio at night, so we could be alone. I just have to have him, and that is it. Soul of mine, I call him.

This morning all we talked about was horses.

Of course I told him that Espiritu is without equal, the most beautiful horse in all the Land. To that he said, "I will find a horse as beautiful as she is, no matter if I have to import ten thousand of them!"

How much of his numbers are exaggerations, no one knows, because nobody really challenges a king. Of course, he says that's what he likes about me. I do challenge him, and make him think. I teach him things I have learned, about the healing properties of plants, and the order of the stars, and things like that. I even sometimes write outlines of things to discuss.

Look at what we have covered:

The Structure of the World

The Beginning, End, and Middle of the Times

The Cycles of the Years and Positions of Stars

Nature and Instincts of the Animals

The Alternations of Solstices and Seasons

The Art of Thought, and the Power of Human Mental Processes

The Varieties and Medicinal Properties of Plants

Things Hidden and Invisible

And my personal favorites, the Elements of Earth, Water, Wind, and Fire. (Book of Wisdom 7: 17-21 New Jerusalem Bible)

He told me one time he was eager to build a house beautiful enough for all of us to dwell in. Dad gave him the go-ahead (after denying the right to his father David. Dad said David had shed too much blood to build a house of peace). So Solomon got the contract and he and the Triple A have been very busy getting all the details done around that.

I have to say that I don't mind him doing this, as it brings him to the Gate more often. He certainly loves working with all the craftsmen and the jewels.

▪ ▪ ▪

Solomon once said the only jewels that mattered to him were those reflected in my eyes. (Sigh.)

Lately, I'm not so sure that is true anymore.

He isn't coming to meet me as often as he used to… says he is getting really busy. I hope this Temple contract doesn't go to his head and cause him to forget me.

▪ ▪ ▪

Chapter Fifteen

Well, guess what. The Temple is finally finished, and we had a giant celebration. It was the first time I remember we all left the Ranch and went into the Valley. It was quite the affair, with sacrifices (which Mom hates) and people praying and clapping and cheering. Dad arrived in a giant cloud, which seemed to please the crowd, and it was all in all a really good day. Dad came back humming. Mom confided to me that she hopes this lasts, because the Valley Landers have a history of short term commitments to projects in general and relationships with us in particular.

Tonight I learned that Solomon has decided to build his own house and make it quite spectacular. He is bringing in even more contractors than he used for the Temple and says it is going to take nearly twice as long to build. Mom and I see this as a very bad sign. How could one Valley Lander need a house bigger than a Temple?

He isn't talking to me as often, except sporadically to say "Hi" whenever he sees me at the Gate when he walks by. He is hanging out now with a group I don't even recognize. Mom calls it his "entourage." I can't help but notice that there are some very attractive women with him, laughing and calling out his name. One of them pretended to stumble and he reached out to "support her." She got all blushy and giggled, and I noticed his chest sort of puffing up. (Hers already was.) I am not feeling good about this at all.

I keep calling out to him, but he barely looks in my direction. I cannot and will not chase him. Dad says that is unseemly, and not the Rancher's way.

"Soul of Mine," I call him in my bed at night. I remember the scent of his morning ointment, rubbed on his face like mints and spices. He told me I was beautiful—more beautiful than pearls, or little lambs skipping through a pasture. I was well prepared to run away with him, even leave the Ranch to be in his presence.

As it turns out, I am sad to say that Soul of Mine ended up being so long gone. One day he didn't show up at all. Looking back on it, I realize that the signs were there. He had begun to come to see me less and less frequently. I knew he was busy of course, being king and all.

He had duties and cases to decide. I even helped him with one about two women who were both claiming to be the mother of a child. He asked my advice and I told him to always let the heart decide. He came up with a very clever solution to a seemingly impossible case. He began to write our thoughts down.

You can read more about this, if you like, in our jointly published book called Song of Solomon.

We actually wrote several books together. Our most famous is called Proverbs, but there were others like The Book of Wisdom and Ecclesiastes. He wrote that last one after we had already broken up. You can tell by some of the verses he wrote that he was feeling very down. "Vanity, vanity all things are vanity" certainly wasn't inspired by me. It must have been one of his many girlfriends who used her looks to get him to give her things and then drifted away.

Breaking up was not my idea either.

He just stopped coming to see me. I was frantic at first. Was he hurt? Or worse? Had he fallen out of his chariot? Surely only injury or death could have kept him from me.

But as one day stretched into two, then three, I began to realize that he wasn't going to show up anymore. My waiting was in vain.

No matter how loudly I called out, "Solomon, here I am," he just couldn't hear me. I am not sure why.

Chattanango said he had seen Solomon spending more and more time with Skinner. At first Skinner just brought him jewels and then a mirror. Then there was the Queen of Sheba, who showered him with so many presents they could hardly count them all. She came a long way for his turkey sandwich, is all I can say.

Q said he heard that Skinner would steal into Solomon's room while he was asleep, dropping little melted gold drops in his ears. I don't know if that really happened. I just know that soon Solomon couldn't hear me anymore.

The other Ranch Hands would talk, but Chattanango didn't want to hurt my feelings. They say that Solomon fell in love with a thousand other voices.

Was it because I couldn't touch him? Was it because he couldn't hear me? Taste my kisses with his mouth? If only I could become visible to him, maybe that would change things!

I took out one of his letters to me. There was no date at the top, but I knew it had been one of his early ones. He wrote:

"Beloved,

I have loved and searched for you from my youth. I am determined to have you as my bride. I have fallen in love with your beauty.

Because of your noble birth I can share God's life. Indeed, I realize that you share the secrets of God's knowledge, and make choice of what he will do.

(Book of Wisdom 8: 2-4)

I took out another one. I think this one was written when he had a Greek tutor, because the language sounds a little elevated.

"My Fairest,

I know that I will find noble contentment in your friendship, inexhaustible riches in your activities, understanding in the cultivation of your society, and renown in conversing with you."

(Book of Wisdom: 8: 18-19)

Dad had shown me some of the letters Solomon had written to him too, asking for my hand. I took one out now, and read it again.

"God of our ancestors, Lord of Mercy, you have chosen me to be king over your people, to be judge of your sons and daughters.

With you is Wisdom. She knows your works, she was present when you made the world, she understands what is pleasing in your eyes and what agrees with your commandments. Please send her forth from your throne of glory to help me and to toil with me and teach me what is pleasing to you, since she knows and understands everything. She will guide me prudently in my actions and will protect me with her glory.

Then all I do will be acceptable. I shall govern your people justly and be worthy of my father's throne." (Book of Wisdom 9-11)

■ ■ ■

Chapter Sixteen

The day I finally realized I had been deserted was on a Friday. I had waited at the Gate all morning and afternoon. I didn't even eat anything, because I had brought some figs and honey to share with him. But I waited and I waited and nothing. No note. No scent of Solomon. Only silence.

And then I began to realize he wasn't going to come at all. The feeling started late in the afternoon. It came on like a pounding and a hammering. I got a tightness around my temple and then …it was like a spear was being thrust in my side. I started gasping for breath and then Chattanango came and scooped me up and said, "No more, Contessa. No more. I can't stand to see you like this."

He carried me up to my room and laid me gently on my bed, then walked out and closed the door. I must have had a terrible night, because when I woke up, I was all tangled up in my bed sheets.

That night, the last night Soul of Mine did not show up at all, Mom came into the room and sat beside me. She gently stroked my hair and wiped the tears that were falling. "There there, Contessa. I know it hurts. Believe me, Dad and I both know the pain that you are feeling."

I just continued to sob, burying my face in my pillow. "He said he loved me, but now he ignores me. Was it all a lie?"

As she sat on the bed looking at me, I suddenly got up and went over to my desk. I took out a pen and a piece of paper and wrote "Dear Jess. Beware of the Valley Landers. They will break your heart. Tess."

I folded it up and hurried out the door. I called Q and gave him the letter. "Please take this out and slip it under the Gate. Be quick about it."

I could only hope that Jess would get my message before it was too late.

▪ ▪ ▪

It was shortly after that I heard him. I was down at Crystal Lake, trying to forget my broken heart when I heard it—muffled at first, then it grew into a wail that rocked my very soul.

"Eloi, Eloi, lama sabachtani!"

I reached for my backpack and began to run. Q flew up beside me. "Where are you going?" he asked. "It's Jess! He needs me!" I yelled. "Here are your directions," Q said. "We knew this day would come."

When I reached the Gate I began to spin. I felt the fire of passion and hurt, longing and love rising inside me as I began to fall in what seemed like a thousand flames.

▪ ▪ ▪

Fia felt a jolt go through her. Tiny light pulses began reverberating behind her eyes. She wondered if it might be due to her fall, yet oddly she was beginning to feel a tingling strength returning. She rubbed her head a moment, stretched, and continued to read.

▪ ▪ ▪

Part Two:
THE VALLEY

Chapter Seventeen

I landed in a small crowded room. I could hear voices talking in different languages. Light was flickering above their heads.

I slowly got my bearings to discover I was in a media room like Dad's, but this one had lots of seats in it, and the screen was one dimensional, with subtitles. As a series of continuous on-screen explosions took place, a bearded man moved over to sit beside me, and whispered, "Why are you here?" "Jess," I said. "Excellent," he replied. He handed me a packet. "This packet holds everything you will need. You will find in it a key to your hotel room. A map and bus pass are included. Here is a letter I am supposed to give you, before taking my leave."

"Wait, before you go. Where am I?" I asked, rubbing the knot on my head. "Welcome to Hollywood, Contessa!" he said with a smile and then disappeared.

"Hollywood?" I repeated as I made my way into the sunlight. I thought the map I had studied said Holy Woods! "That Q!" I shouted in frustration. When will he ever slow down enough to get the details right?

I sat on a bench outside the theatre and noticed people's handprints in the cement. Jess and I used to do that in the mud around Crystal Lake, I recalled, and suddenly a wave of homesickness came over me.

I felt like a rock was crushing my chest. I opened the letter and recognized the handwriting at once. Only Jess would sign his initial J with a little fish hook on it.

Dear Tess,

Thank you for coming when I called. Your work is to complete the work I started. I know you will do it well. Love, Jess

P.S. I hear the deli on Sunset makes a great tuna sandwich.

See you soon.

J

▪ ▪ ▪

I took the map, found the bus, and made it to my hotel. When I entered the room, the stale darkness matched the heaviness in my heart.

I quickly shed my clothes, which smelled somewhat of liquid gel, and climbed under the shower. As I closed my eyes, I imagined being under the waterfall at the Ranch. I willed myself to hear every drop saying, "You are my Beloved."

I fell on the bed exhausted and slept for I didn't know how long. Was it one day or two? Or a century? Time here seemed to move much more slowly than it does on the Ranch. I looked at the flicking numbers on the clock, looked out at the traffic that was just starting outside, and got up to get dressed.

When I opened the closet I was relieved to find an entire wardrobe there, handpicked for me by Chattanango and Mom.

I had mostly worn blue jeans on the Ranch, but apparently my work here was going to require more outfits. Of that, I was very sure.

I propped myself up on my bed, got out my notebook, and began to write. Mom had always said, "When you don't know what else to do, write something."

So I got busy and wrote all night. I must have fallen asleep with my clothes on, because a flashing green alarm went off right next to me. The sound of it was horrible! We would never wake up like that on the Ranch.

But I was here, I remembered, in the Valley, and I had work to do. I got up, took a quick shower, arranged my hair in a ponytail, and headed across the street, where a familiar aroma was drawing me to a crowded enclosure where people were standing in line out the door. I listened carefully to their orders.

When I got to the counter to order there I repeated what the lady in front of me had said.

"I will have a double latte vodka valium mochiatto, please."

The server looked at me and said, "Excuse me?" "Isn't that what she just ordered?" I asked. "Yeah, but she's a comedian," the barista said. "Oh, well, then suggest something." "The double espresso mocha is one of our favorites here." "Sounds good, I'll try it." I observed people exchanging pieces of paper and coins for their cups of coffee. Again, I was relieved at the thoughtfulness of Chattanango and Mom in packing for me. My saddlebag, which had been replaced by a messenger bag worn over my shoulders, had plenty of green papers in it. I reached in and handed one to the server. His eyes got really wide and said, "Miss, we can't make change for a million-dollar bill here."

"I'll help her out," said the man behind me. I turned to face him, and saw a man with a deep forehead, with one comb-over strand of hair. "My name is Dick," he said. "Welcome to Hollywood." "My name is Tessa," I said, responding. "Thank you for helping me out there."

"I can tell you are not from around here."

"You would be right. I'm just visiting," I said.

"Business or pleasure?" he asked.

"Do I have to choose?" I smiled. At last, here was someone who was actually interested in getting to know me.

He offered me a place to sit down beside him.

"What do you do here?" I asked.

"Agent Slash Consultant Slash Director. Just like everybody else here, these days, except I don't have a script I'm trying to sell."

"I'll bet you stay very busy," I said.

"Never busy enough. And you?"

"I work for our family business. I'm just in town to finish up the work my brother started."

"What kind of family business?" Dick asked.

"Farming. Ranching. Development. A mixture of things, really."

"Well, let me know if I can help you. I have friends in low places," joked Dick, handing me his card.

Suddenly he stopped and said, "You know, that million dollar bill is going to create problems for people. If you like, I can walk you across the street to a banker I know, and she will set up an account for you. That way you can draw down money in much smaller bills."

"That would be lovely," I said, following him out the door.

He introduced me to the bank president, named Judith, who stood up immediately from her desk when she saw Dick standing beside me. She was very friendly, and at one point nodded to a cartoon a customer had drawn of her, holding a big bag of coins. The caption read, "You bring it. I Carry It!" I looked at the name tag on her desk. "Judith I. Carriet." Somehow that name seemed familiar to me, but I couldn't quite place it. I signed all the paperwork she presented, which they each then signed too. She gave me a large envelope full of green bills as well as a debit card. Dick and I walked out the door, shook hands, and went our separate ways.

▪ ▪ ▪

There is something very different about Contessa, Dick thought. It is a combination of friendliness and power, innocence and intelligence. He had never quite seen that shade of gold in a skin tone, either. He was going to keep a close eye on her, for sure.

She also was surrounded by an incredible fragrance. What was it? Just the hint of roses? No, even better than that. It was the one he had been raised from childhood to detect. It was the scent of money. This lady could make a man very wealthy indeed, he realized, and Dick intended to be the one she did.

▪ ▪ ▪

Chapter Eighteen

I spent the better part of today day wandering around L.A.

My hopes had soared when I saw that Los Angeles stood for The City of Angels. But one stroll down Sunset Boulevard told me it was in name only. There seemed to be no angels here standing on street corners.

I walked until my feet hurt. Finally, I spotted a building that looked a lot like the Library at home. I stepped inside and found I was in a church. I lifted my eyes up to the arching columns, and recognized designs the Triple A had done. They had loved to sketch their ideas upside down on the glass floor in the studio, hoping that Valley Landers would look up and see them.

One man, named Michaelangelo, had been especially good at seeing them, as well as another Italian named Leonardo. What were those columns called?

Oh yes—flying buttresses they called them. Q had giggled at the term when he first heard it but had been silenced with a single look from Algo, head of the Triple A.

The scent of candles soothed me. I leaned back against the wood of the pew and closed my eyes. I dreamed I was back at the Ranch, riding Espiritu. Clouds were parting and rays of hope were streaming in from all sides. I must have fallen asleep because someone shook my shoulder and asked, "Miss, are you awake?" I sat up with a start, remembering now where I was. "I'm sorry" the woman continued. "What is your name?" I asked. "I'm Contessa."

"Luz," she replied. "I have to close the church now because it is getting dark. But you are welcome to come back tomorrow." "Indeed I shall," I said rising. "I like it here."

On my walk back to the hotel I did order a tuna sandwich from the deli Jess had recommended. I carried it into my room in its plain brown bag, sat on the bed, unwrapped it, and ate it very slowly. I was having a hard time swallowing this food, this taste, this place.

The next day, when I went back to church, I found it was very crowded. They were having a funeral there—a very sad thing to behold.

We never have funerals on the Ranch, as no one ever dies there.

I wished that I could tell the people crying that it was going to be okay. I wished that I could share with them the lesson Mom gave me and Jess, early one morning.

She had taken us to the garden, and showed us little caterpillars. One was striped with yellow and black lines. "Like the tigers!" Jess had said. "I liked the combination, and decided to carry it through," said Mom, smiling. Then she directed us to the little caterpillar again. She told us to sit and watch.

This little worm crawled up a twig and began to spin a cocoon. It completely encased itself until there was no more worm to see, only an encased jewel dangling on the branch.

Mom said, "Do you know what is happening on the inside, even though it is dead looking on the outside?" We had to admit we didn't know. "Sleeping?" we guessed finally, and she smiled. "Very close. Right now this little creature is giving up the form it once had in order to accept a new one. This time with wings."

She said, "Let's come back in a little while, and see what is happening." We did, and we watched in amazement as this dangling chrysalis turned into a butterfly.

"Someday, Jess, the same thing is going to happen to you," she said gently. "They will wrap you up very tightly and lay you in a deep dark place. But your sleep will not last. You will emerge and ascend into the sky."

I leaned forward from my seat and whispered to the weeping parents in front of me, "She is not dead. She is sleeping." But I don't think they heard me because their crying was so very loud. When they approached the casket, someone walked up to them and whispered, "It's over. You will never see her again." And then I heard him snarl to the mother in an even lower tone, "Of course, this is all your fault." Immediately, I recognized the voice. It was Skinner, acting as a pall bearer, making a way into the middle of their grief.

Skinner. What a jerk! How can they even begin to know what a liar he is? The people filed out and Skinner just winked at me as he walked by. Apparently, he knew where I was, and was determined to shadow my every move.

▪ ▪ ▪

The next day I awoke again, smelling coffee. I decided the Valley Land did have its consolations, with that smell being one of them. I pulled on my jeans and hoodie, grabbed my messenger bag, put on my boots, and headed off to the coffee shop on the corner.

I ordered my now favorite double espresso mocha, took a seat by a window, got out my journal, and prepared to sip my way into the day, favorite pen in hand. I had written for about twenty minutes when guess who showed up again. "Dick," he said extending his hand. "You remember me from the other day?"

"Yes, of course," I said, inviting him to join me. Hospitality had been a very big part of the Ranch, and I certainly wasn't going to forget my manners now.

He looked out the window at the people streaming by, sipping his double mochiatto. "This place is really something, isn't it?" he commented, shaking his head. I didn't say anything, deciding to listen carefully to what he was saying.

"What are you writing?" He leaned over, glancing at my journal.

"Just some lessons I've learned from the family business. Some ideas I've had since I've been here."

"How long have you been gone?" he asked, looking up at me in what I suppose he thought was an attractive pose.

"It feels like thousands of years, actually, when I think about it. So, I don't," I said, covering my journal now, protectively.

That morning, while I was standing in the shower, I had figured out a simple formula for creating water out of ashes. I had just jotted it down in my notebook. I thought this might help people here with problems of drought they were experiencing.

I also had been formulating a design for harnessing wind power, knowing what I did about Espiritu and the way she moves.

The smog in L.A. was going to choke them all off someday, and I was concerned.

The biggest one on my mind was how to reduce solar power to the size of a grain of sand. I figured that maybe if I kept up in the Valley what I would usually be doing at the Ranch, talking through designs and creations with Dad, Mom and the Triple A, maybe I wouldn't be so lonely.

Still, I wasn't quite ready to share these ideas. I had to find someone with a pure heart, and I was pretty sure Dick was not the one.

"You know, Tess, I've got to tell you. I see a lot of people come in here, and I've never met anyone like you," he said, pushing back his chair. I knew a fishing line when I heard it and did not take the bait.

"Am I right in thinking that when your work is done here, you will get to go home?"

"Yes, that is correct," I said.

"Well, from what I just saw glancing over at your journal, your work could help a lot of people. You would like to do that, wouldn't you?

"Of course," I replied.

"Why don't you come to my studio, and let me record your thoughts. Then I will shop them around for us, of course, so that everyone can benefit."

I politely declined and took my leave. This Dick character was not to be trusted. Of that, I was sure.

▪ ▪ ▪

Chapter Nineteen

I decided that the most logical way to accomplish my mission would be to go to the place that had Jess' name in lights. I got my journal, put on a comfortable pair of pants, and headed over to "The First Church Mart of Jesus."

I walked through the parking lot, came to the information desk, introduced myself, and asked to meet with the leader. I told them I had an important message to share with their people. I was quickly directed downstairs to "Women's Ministries." I made my way through the labyrinth and found a small sign over a door which read: Nursery/Sunday School/Volunteer Recruitment/ Women's Ministries. The hand-lettered sign on the door said: "Contact: Overa Xtended." All these departments were run by one part-time worker, Overa, who told me that, unfortunately, she had no budget for hiring, but would I like to volunteer?

I agreed and was given a badge to wear. "Your job," she carefully explained to me, "is to greet the customers with a smile and direct them to the appropriate aisle." "Did you just say customers?" I asked. "Yes, we call them customers so we can keep in mind that they always have a choice about where and what to buy."

Looking forward to my first day volunteering, I showed up early and was thrilled when I saw car after car heading into the huge parking lot. Tempers occasionally flared when someone tried to cut in line, and a fight almost broke out when an elderly lady 'stole' the designated parking spot of a large man in a Hummer with a bumper sticker that read "I love Jesus. Up Yours." Security guards had to be called over when the woman began cursing and trying to hit the man with her purse. Despite the commotion, cars just swerved around them in the quest to get as close as possible to the door.

As I walked past the nursery, I noticed a sign that read, "Bloom where you are planted."

I know from working in the garden, however, that plants can't just bloom wherever they are planted. For example, an orchid planted in a desert could not bloom no matter how much it tried. Mom said each plant needs particular conditions for it to thrive, and that is what gardeners and husbandmen are for, to help the plants flourish. I figured I would talk to Overa after the service and suggest modifications to the quote on the door.

I tried cheering myself up with, "This is going to be great! I love calling others to come and learn." As the crowds began to rush in, however, I found that learning was not on their minds. "Where can we find the entertainment section?" asked a woman with her frowning husband in tow, who was still clutching a golf club in his right hand. I prepared to ask her why she came to a church for entertainment, when Overa stepped up and said, "Aisle 1." She then turned to me, handing me a chart. "I forgot to give you this when you signed up. Don't talk please. Just direct them to the appropriate location. This crowd likes to get in and get out."

The chart listed: Aisle 1: Entertainment, Aisle 2: New Mate, Aisle 3: Get Rich, Aisle 4: Why We Are Number One. "End

Times" material was located appropriately on the last aisle. All other requests were directed to the Gift Shop, which featured prominent selections by the preacher himself, as well as key chains, earrings, and other paraphernalia. "I'll bet Jess would hate this," I thought to myself as I surveyed the merchandise.

Exactly two minutes before the doors opened, the preacher, his ushers, and a host of others gathered us all together for prayer.

"Dear Lord, You know our needs are many. Our media costs alone are huge. We ask that you lay it upon the people's hearts to honor You, Lord, yes You, as they make their checks out to Church Mart this day."

With that, he looked proudly upon the gleaming cars in the parking lot, and asked in a low voice "Have we gotten a count yet?" One man stepped forward and whispered, "Five thousand four hundred and seventy one." "Excellent," the pastor smiled and then turned toward us volunteers, and said "Ok, folks, it's Show Time!"

The newly installed three million dollar pipe organ began blasting out "I Come to the Garden Alone." The electronically controlled doors swung open, and the crowd began streaming in, faces intent on their goals, their "eyes on the prize."

People grabbed their carts, and quickly headed down the aisles, installing their headphones as they went. I watched in amazement as they listened to the preacher on the giant screen while loading their carts. Instead of clapping they just snapped their fingers, as "studies have shown it is easier and faster, and keeps one hand free for credit cards," whispered Overa proudly.

When I tried to stop and talk to a man as he was leaving, asking why he had made the selections he did, I was quickly cut off by my director, who was now holding a baby on each hip since they were "low on help in the nursery." She pulled me aside, and, after looking left and right, quickly ripped off my badge with her teeth, since that was the only free appendage she had. "I can see that you are not going to fit in here. Disturbing the customers with questions is not allowed! We love you, and don't come back," she snarled, spitting my badge onto the floor. She then spun on her heels and lunged back into the crowd, each baby leaning back at a forty five degree angle due to the velocity and ferocity with which she traveled. She shouted into her headset, "I'm on my way!" She plowed through the crowd to thc "Caribbean Cruise With Pastor" registration table, which was being swamped with sign-ups.

Suddenly, I saw him. I called out "Soul of Mine!" and turned to reach out to him, just as the security guards approached. I saw him smile, slap his hands on the back of several men nearby, and begin handing out business cards. I overheard the words "deal of a lifetime" before the security guards quickly and not too gently escorted me off the property. As I was struggling to stay upright one of them managed to stuff a "Voter's Guide" down my blouse. It was pre-checked, and offered a 20% off discount coupon to the Gift Store. One of the guards, apparently feeling badly about how I was being treated, whispered to me, "I hear they need some volunteers at Six Flags over Jesus. Things might work out for you there."

As I made my way slowly back to my apartment, I realized that this work was going to be harder, and take much longer, than even Jess had imagined.

Now the loneliness doesn't just hit me when I walk into my hotel room. It follows me around daily. I can't stop thinking about the Ranch, wondering what Jess is doing now that he is back. I wonder how Q is coming along in his quest to make Triple A. I remembered the last time I saw him, when Q came knocking on my door late one night. "Tess, I'm sorry to wake you up, but I am so excited!"

"What is it Q?" I asked, rubbing my eyes. "Well, you know how your Dad pointed out that book to me, A BRIEF HISTORY BEFORE TIME? I looked up my own history and discovered that I am from the angel group that saw the light flash when Skinner left. Even though we were warned by Gabriel to look away, some of us sort of peeked. Some of us meaning me. As a result, I got the condition known as 'discloudsia,' which means I have a hard time distinguishing dark from light. That's why I have a hard time sorting the clouds!"

"Q, that is terrific!" I enthused, slapping him delightedly in the space between his wings. "Now what are you going to do about it?" "Well, your Mom promised to work with me on a daily basis, helping me distinguish shades of gray. She said it will take some time, but if I work hard at it, I will soon be able to graduate from the laundry! Besides, your Dad has been getting kind of grumpy lately, wearing only dark clouds."

"Anything else?" I asked, getting ready to cuddle back down into my fluffy bed. "Yes. I have to do a design project for review by the Triple A. I'm going to start on it tomorrow."

"Good work, Q," I murmured sleepily. "And good night."

That was the last I saw of him for about a week. Then he came bursting in and shouted, "I've got it! Please come to the demonstration at the studio tomorrow at noon, okay?"

"Okay," I promised. As we all gathered at the table, Q said, "You know how the Valley Landers always say thank you before they eat, but most of us know they don't really mean it? Well, I have designed this little device, called the Gastronomic Authenticity Genometer, or GAG for short. It will go off whenever a Valley Lander doesn't really mean what they are praying."

Dad just rolled his eyes, and looked over at Mom, who said gently, "Q, that is a great idea. But I think we already know when Valley Landers really mean what they are praying. Why don't you work a little harder to come up with something we all really need?" That was the last I saw of Q, because soon after that he was flying beside me as I was running toward the Gate. Of course, I later realized, he had blurred the words of my destination when writing them down. Hopefully, by now, however, he was on his way to the Triple A, while I was in L.A., finishing the work my brother had started.

▪ ▪ ▪

Chapter Twenty

I began the next day as I did every day, getting up early. I hiked the canyon areas, calling out to people, but nobody came over. They all had little ear plugs stuck in their ears, and never seemed to hear me. After my walk I came home, showered, and then begin walking the city again, trying to find someone to listen to what I have to say. As usual, during these long walks, I thought about life on the Ranch. Like how Mom is always giving gifts, for no apparent reason. I remember coming back from the Library one day to find Mom sitting on the front porch, smiling from ear to ear. She said:

"Tessa, close your eyes and hold out your hand." I did, and felt her putting something on my finger. I opened my eyes and was astonished to find the Rings of Saturn hovering in perfect symmetry on my right hand. A better word than "on" would be "around," as nothing really touched my skin. She said, "Your father and I created it yesterday, with you in mind. We wanted it to be multi colored, like the rainbow you designed, and we also wanted it to be magnificent and spectacular, as you are. I didn't want it to be heavy or get in the way of your writing, which is why I decided to make the peripheral bands hover and swirl, weightlessly. Do you like it?" "Mom," I said, hurling myself into her lap, "I shall wear this always!" Dad had been standing behind us, beaming, and I turned and flung myself into his arms.

I looked down now at my empty hand, knowing the ring does not show up in this atmosphere. I could feel it humming and swirling, however, in perpetual reminder, of my parent's love for me. It was because of this absence, I suppose, that I went walking along, glancing in jewelry stores.

I was noticing that some of the rubies and pearls in the windows were the same as the ones that line the roads to the Ranch. The opal, especially, caught my eye, as it reflected the exact luminescent colors of Crystal Lake. I walked inside to take a closer look at the stone, when I lifted my head and saw him. Solomon, my beloved. Only now apparently his name was "Suleiman." So said the sign on the counter.

There was someone else ahead of me, wearing a business suit. One glance at the slick polish on the hair, and I knew it was Skinner. If he knew I was there, he pretended he didn't. He just kept talking.

"So what I am telling you, Sully, is that if you leverage your jewels here in the case, as well as those in your vault, you—I mean we—can buy a whole diamond mine."

"How is that possible?" asked Sully, never taking his eyes off the ring on Skinner's hand. It must have seemed somehow familiar to him. I looked at it, and knew it instantly. It was the same one Aaron had made when he got tired of waiting for Moses to come down from the mountain after talking with Dad. He and his group had gotten so impatient that they decided to make up some stupid looking bull god of their own. This ring was the result.

I thought it had been destroyed in the fire, but apparently someone salvaged it. Now Skinner had it, wearing it proudly and flashing it around.

It was solid gold, made in the image of a bull. It had two diamond eyes, two black onyx stones for nostrils, and a ruby in its mouth for a tongue. Its two horns were carved of jasper. It was huge. And ugly. "Some have more time than taste," Mom had once said, and looking at that atrocity, I had to agree.

"Where did you get that ring?" Sully asked.

"I got it at Aaron's discount store," Skinner laughed, trying to keep Sully's mind on the task at hand.

"No, you didn't," Sully said. "I've seen that ring before. It was written about as far back as Moses."

"Listen, Sully, tell you what I'll do," said Skinner, interrupting. "You sign this deed here to Suleiman Jewelers over to me and we'll buy the diamond mine together, ok? If you do that, I will give you this ring."

"Don't do it, Solomon," I whispered. But he did not hear.

Sully paused, wanting it badly but apparently still enough of a businessman to look for the details. "And how can this little jewelry store buy an entire diamond mine?"

"Don't worry about the details. I've got the fine print covered. It's a leveraging process I've designed called derivatives," smiled Skinner, as he held up the ring. Sully quickly scribbled his name and the ring was his. "You remind me of your cousin, Esau," said Skinner as he took the deed and turned to go. "He signed away his rights, too. And what a deal he got."

As he walked past he whispered, "Hello Contessa. These Valley Landers sell themselves so cheaply!" He paused, cocked his head a little bit and then said with a smile, "Oddly enough, I feel like getting a bowl of soup. Care to join me?"

I shook my head and just stood there, shocked that Solomon had done this. What about the proverb we had written down together, about sudden wealth leading to poverty? Had he forgotten every pearl I had ever shared?

"Solomon," I called out softly, the name getting stuck in my throat. He did not respond. "Solomon!" I said it again, this time louder and with more urgency.

He never looked up from that ring. "I'm sorry Miss, the store is closed." He turned back to a woman laughing in the background and called out, "Poopsie, I think I just made us a fortune!"

I heard the little bell on the back of his door chime as he slammed the door shut. "He didn't even see me," I said to myself. "What will it take to get his attention?" I began to ponder these things as I walked down the street trying to find something to eat.

I was really hungry now. And of course, it made me remember cooking at the Ranch and how Dad loves to cook.

He stirs up the most amazing concoctions. He is fearless in his creations and will throw anything into the mix. We all try to eat up everything on our plates at supper, because if we don't, it will show up in the omelette the next morning. Sometimes it works, sometimes it doesn't. My least favorite combo was the hummus omelettes. Sometimes he puts everything into a crusted bowl and tells Jess to take it out to the shepherds.

He also loves to make Prophet's stew, which can sometimes have a bitter taste to it, in my opinion. Almost without exception, when we are all in the kitchen, Mom will pass through, lean over, taste it, and say, "This needs a little more spice." Once when she said this I heard Dad laugh to himself, "En la cocina como la cama," or something to that effect. "In the kitchen as in the bedroom," was what he was saying.

Dad's humming made me remember how we could hear the Ranch Hands singing when we were doing the dishes. In fact, most of the Ranch Hands could not only work--but sing. Tabby Nackle, the one in charge of the choir, invited me to join in with them on Wednesday nights. She said I had a special knack for harmonizing.

Jess also tried out for the choir. After practice Tabby took him aside and said, "You know, I think your gifts would be better served by hanging out in the kitchen—maybe learning how to cater large events." So Jess went over to see Chuy at the Culinary Institute, who knew how to make a little bit of food go a long, long way.

Both Dad and Mom felt it was important that we each develop our own hobbies (and maybe give them some free time too.) They said they didn't raise us to be shadows, but wanted us very much to learn to develop our own lives and minds.

▪ ▪ ▪

Dad loves speaking different kinds of languages, and I have definitely picked that up. Sometimes we like to sit and make up languages that nobody understands but him and me. It is sort of our secret thing.

▪ ▪ ▪

Chapter Twenty-One

This is the passage I just found in my journal, sitting here on my hotel sofa in Hollywood. After reading it, I looked over at the two-burner cooktop, with its little microwave up top. I got up and went over to look in the pantry, finding some packaged popcorn. I popped it into the microwave, and as I reached for the salt, tears come to my eyes. Jess's solution to every kitchen dilemma was "Add more salt."

I opened the door to the microwave and put the little popped kernels in my mouth, hoping that eating something would cheer me up. But nothing here in the Valley tastes the same.

I don't think they have enough flavors.

I decided to go sit in the church and take comfort in the light streaming in from the multicolored windows.

▪ ▪ ▪

Returning to the church that has become familiar to me now, I sat near the front, closest to the candles. A choir boy was singing, sweet high notes and pure. It reminded me of the summer nights when we all would gather at the Gate and listen to David's songs. I was so moved by the music that I began to approach the altar, trying to get closer to the source of the sound.

And then I heard a voice I knew all too well.

"Tess, I knew you'd show up. But I figured it might take you longer to find me."

"I wasn't looking for you," I said. "I was looking for the last place Jess was before he left."

"Oh, you won't find that here!" Skinner laughed. "Right after that magnificent death scene—oh the glory—oh the blood—he disappeared and the crowds were so confused. I stepped right in and said, 'Here's what you need to do. You need to each form your own denominations, with your very own set of rules.' Well, it has pretty much created a gory history, don't you think? Oh, and how do you like how I added, 'Be sure to say that Daddy likes yours best!'" While he was talking he had sidled up closer beside me. Suddenly his hand clamped over my mouth. His robed arm reached around from behind me, and he dragged me, kicking, down the aisle and back into the alley. I could taste the sweat on his hand as he forced it against my mouth. While his right hand covered my mouth, his knee smashed into my thigh. His left hand started moving up my leg. "You and your mother," he spat. "So precious. So perfect. So beautiful. But always just out of my reach." Suddenly, I shoved the heel of my hand against his nose, as Chattanango had taught me to do.

Skinner gasped in pain and then came back at me. He slammed me against the wall, his foul breath right in front of my lips. I turned my head out from under his hand and asked calmly, in a monotone voice, "Where did you get the priest's robe, Skinner? It makes you look flabby."

He recoiled at the insult to his appearance and released me.

"You'd be surprised, Tess, as perhaps your brother was, at how little these people look beyond appearances. You would also be amazed at the number of disguises I wear and the authority I get so easily with them. I'm in business, politics, government, the media, you name it. Skinner Enterprises is everywhere!"

He righted his white collar that had gotten twisted during our struggle. "You can have no leadership in this place. I've worked hard to see to that. I'm done with you for now, Contessa." With that, he turned back towards the balcony.

I walked out of the church and made my way back toward my hotel room. I stripped away my clothes, which smelled like a mixture of incense and acid, and climbed into the shower. I turned on the water as hot as it would go and leaned my head against the white tile squares. I needed to feel clean again… to wash it all away. I just stood there for a long, long time and let the water fall.

▪ ▪ ▪

The next day I had to get away. I went down to the Union Train Station and bought a train ticket to a dude ranch I'd seen advertised in a brochure. I hoped the rocking motion of the train would remind me of being in Mom's lap when I was a little girl. I yearned for the simplicity of one track laid out beside the other, in perfect equidistance as far as the eye could see—one track called Truth, and the other Beauty… tracks that could carry me back in my mind to the Ranch again.

The train's engine snorted, and the train lurched forward as I leaned my head against the glass. I began trying to remember everything Jess had said to me. Everything Mom had told me.

What did Dad sound like in the morning when he gave his first yawning roar? I remembered how in the late afternoon he would walk in the door and yell, "Hello everybody! I'm home!"

As I looked out onto the furrowed fields the train was passing, I remembered when I first got to open the gates to the irrigation. It had happened as a result of the dinosaur fiasco.

One day Mom looked out over the ruins left by Dinah and T-Rex's unfortunate demise and said, "I think I can grow a garden here—a much larger one." The challenge was getting the water from our single well out into the fields.

Her garden would definitely need Living Water.

Dad brought the problem to the Triple A, who designed a series of trenches and underground pools that could be gathered at the surface and then trenched out to the field.

We all stood there looking at the rows of sunflowers seeds Mom had planted. As the water swirled past us in a ditch Dad nodded over at me and Jess. I will never forget the sight of the water rushing into the field as our hands lifted up the gate.

"Everything will live where the water goes," Dad mused, leaning on his shovel with Jess and me standing by his side. Mom reached over and gave him a kiss, saying, "I will be able to grow so much beauty here, thanks to you, My Love."

Then of course Jess and I took off running down the rows—chasing each other joyously and splashing the warm water into the sky.

▪ ▪ ▪

I remembered how Dad would toss his hat onto the hook on the far wall, never missing. One of my favorite things on the Ranch is Dad's hat. It is a dark brown suede cowboy hat with a braided leather hat band. I made the band for him one afternoon with Chattanango's help, and Dad said, "This is beautiful! Thank you, Contessa. I shall wear it with pride." He sat right down and put it around the crown, and I felt like I could burst with joy. He stood up then and modeled it, turning his head this way and that, and we all cracked up laughing. It made him look serious, and handsome, and hardworking, all at the same time.

It now has sweat stains all around the inside, because Dad is always out working the Ranch or out walking the fields. He laughed one time, "If I wasn't born to do this I would have been born again just to make sure I did!" I asked him why he didn't wear a fancier hat to show how important he is. (I knew from watching WECU that Valley Landers, who were trying to be the boss of everything, were especially obsessed with crowns.) Dad just harrumphed and said, "The bigger the crown they want, the more empty their heads must be, needing something heavy to hold them down."

On one of our daily walks he showed me the many uses his hat has. He said, "Well, Contessa, what happens if I come across a stray that is lost and thirsty? Why, I just take my hat off, dip it into a stream, and bring it over for the little one. How would I do that with a big fancy crown? Everything would leak right through!"

As we kept walking he continued, "If I want to take a nap, I just pull the brim down low, lean up against the fence post, and catch a few winks when I'm tired. Everybody deserves a zone of privacy now and then. Try to do that with a crown. One, you'd poke your eye out, and two, there is no zone of privacy for those who wear a crown."

As we walked further, I could tell he was warming to the lessons he was teaching me.

"Or let's say you want to get into a game the Ranch Hands are playing. You just take your hat off and toss it into the ring, and you're in! If you did that with your crown, everybody might stop the game and rush to grab it and then all the fun would be over."

"A good hat also helps you remember things," he smiled, pointing to a little note Mom had jotted down and left in the hat band. He reached up, pulled out the note and read it: 'Beloved, have I told you lately that I adore you?' "You can see why I carry this one around," he said with a smile and tucked it back in the band.

They have a picture of me when I was little, trying on Dad's hat. All you can see is my little body wearing a bathrobe and fluffy slippers, with a big hat sitting on my shoulders. The caption reads, "Someday she'll grow into this." Jess snapped the photo with his first camera. It is framed now on the wall.

How I miss those walls, I thought, as the train clacked and swayed through the fields. As I gazed out the window, I saw a couple out working in the rows. The way they were bent over looked familiar to me. For a moment I thought I might have even seen them at the Ranch. I sat up straighter in my seat as the steward came by for my ticket. "Looking out over there? Migrant workers, probably. Nobody wants their job for sure," he said, scanning my ticket. "How many are there?" I asked. "Millions," he replied.

■ ■ ■

Chapter Twenty-Two

The trip to the Dude ranch did not fill my emptiness. The corrals were so small that the animals barely had room to turn around. The trails were short and littered with trash. And all of the horses looked too sad to ride, standing with their heads practically resting on the ground. I didn't want to add to their misery. How long until I could ride Espiritu again, I wondered. Her hooves ate up the trails. Not so with this herd.

Instead, I ate lunch on the patio, swatting away the flies, and reached for my notebook to sketch out some new ideas I'd gotten on the train. Only, the notebook was gone.

My mind raced back to the place I last had it. I had been at the coffee shop just that morning, and then I walked over to the train station. I remembered some woman had bumped me just as I was getting ready to board the train. She mumbled an apology as she hurried away, and I thought nothing of it. Until now. I quickly boarded the next train out. Who to call? No one. If only Solomon would recognize me again, and take my call. He could have comforted me for a change, I thought to myself as the miles clicked along beneath me.

"Oh well, something good will come of this," I finally said to myself. Something always does. It was the law of the Ranch, and surely it had to apply here.

■ ■ ■

Today, when I returned to my hotel room, I found my notebook. Not where or how I expected. Guess where it was. On-line. My sketches for wind power tunnels. Parts of my journal exposed. My sketches and designs were being downloaded by millions. Suddenly my formulas and designs were circulating around the globe, with the headline: "Who is this genius?"

I was sipping my coffee, contemplating this, when Dick sidled up beside me. "You did this, didn't you," I said, without looking up.

"Can you blame me? Tessa, this is great stuff! It is going to make the world a better place!" He paused, waiting for me to reply. When none came he continued more gently.

"Everyone wants to hear from you now. Isn't that what you wanted? Maybe now you can go home. That is all I really wanted. To help YOU go home."

I looked through him and said nothing.

Dick put his head down, seemingly in shame, but I could see he was emailing someone a photo of me with the heading: "She is the One!"

"How much of a reward did you get?" I asked, standing to leave.

'Ten million plus another thirty thousand if I could get a picture of you. I'm still working a deal with the Saudis on your solar power in a grain of sand idea, which will be huge," he said. "Where is the rest of that formula, by the way? I only want a percentage of everything you create. That's not too much to ask, is it?"

But I knew that Dick would not be satisfied now. Especially when the royalties started pouring in, and when endorsement deals started cropping up. He had trained all his life for this, hadn't he?

And now he wanted more.

▪ ▪ ▪

I had seen a bumper sticker that read: "If you want a friend, get a dog." I decided to take that advice to heart and headed over to the animal shelter. Being around the animals, who had no agenda and wanted nothing from me except love and a hug, was comforting to me. I noticed a little dog who was black with four white paws and a white-tipped tail. So, I immediately filled out the adoption papers and took him home with me. Finally, I had a friend.

This little guy was indeed a blessing. Sometimes, I would hold him and sing to him. Mostly we would walk the paths high in the Hollywood hills. I named him Joshua, because he was willing to walk with me in the wilderness and always knew the way home.

People always left me alone. I had plenty to say, all right. But I had to be asked. That was the rule I had learned on the Ranch. "They have to want to hear you," Mom had said. But people all too rarely looked up from where they were going.

Noticing that L.A. was becoming engulfed in smog, I decided to try to reduce my carbon footprint even more. I bought a blue beach cruiser bike with a wicker basket in it for Joshua, and we used that for trips or just going to the store. I either walked or biked wherever I needed to go.

Wanting to feel productive, I got a job at a local greenhouse. I had moved out of my hotel room into a small studio apartment that allowed pets and had noticed the greenhouse nearby.

The owner hired me on the spot, barely scanning the ID papers Chattanango and Mom had prepared for me. I was happy just to tend to plants. It reminded me of the times with Mom out in the garden. As I studied the soil conditions and the atmosphere, I began jotting many notes on a paper I intended to present to Mom called "The Future of Flowers."

Once, on my break, I thought I saw that couple I had seen before in the fields. This time, they were riding on the back of a truck that was unloading fruit across the street. I did hear some guy call out their names. "Primero," and then "Ultima!" he yelled. "Bring those baskets over here!"

I dashed off a note with my name and contact information and tied it to a rock. I tossed it into the truck as it pulled away.

The next day, I decided to take a tour of some cancer research labs in La Jolla. I took the train down. I got off at Solana Beach and rode my bike the rest of the way in. I had read that San Diego was a leader in life science and biotechnology research and had heard that some of the most advanced cancer research in the world was going on in one square mile in La Jolla. One of the labs was having an open house, and I walked along each row of test tubes and white boards, feeling so at home. At one desk, I saw a small map of the rainforest on the wall. I hung back when the tour turned the corner. I drew a red circle with an arrow pointing to a specific map coordinate, writing, "You will find the plant you need here."

I felt so good walking through that place. It reminded me of home. I couldn't help but wonder why, in the Valley, there were so few research labs in comparison to weapons production factories. I remember Mom being really grumpy about that, saying, "When they fund medical research as much as they do weapons that destroy life, we will help them find cures more quickly."

I wrote in my journal that night: "In the Valley, money seems to flow most naturally toward greed and fear." This makes me very sad. The days dragged on. One time I got out one of the letters Solomon had written to me. After reading it, I folded it up and put it back in my messenger bag. That night I had a dream.

I was lying in bed, and I found myself

reaching for the one I love. I felt as if my heart and soul were wrapped up in him. I looked for him, but he wasn't there.

So I searched through the town, I looked on every street,

but he wasn't there.

I even asked the guards patrolling the town,

"Have you seen the one I love so much?"

Right after that, I found him.

I held him and would not let go

until I had taken him

to the home of my mother. (Song of Songs 3:4)

I awoke, however, to find myself alone in my own bed.

▪ ▪ ▪

The next day Dick tracked me down. I was tending to the orchids when he walked in, wearing a silk shirt, flip flops, and sunglasses. "Hey, Tess, how ya' doing?" he asked.

"Fine," I said simply, focusing on my silent companions.

"Look, Tess, I know you don't like me much, and you don't really need to. But here is the deal. They want you in New York. It is a really HUGE story now—you are the huge story. You are wanted on all the talk shows. The bishop even wants your blessing."

"Not interested," I said, walking right past him.

"Someone named Sol wants to see you," Dick said simply.

I stopped suddenly. "What did you say?"

"Someone named Sol said he would come to meet you in New York."

I sensed that he was probably lying. But the notion of getting out of this place, and maybe meeting a real bishop, someone with power to make a difference, gave me a ray of hope. I decided to take it.

"Ok," I said, "but only if I can take Joshua with me."

"Sure," smiled Dick, beaming now. "We'll give him extra-special attention."

▪ ▪ ▪

Chapter Twenty-Three

When I got to New York, there was a media frenzy. Camera lights flashed in my face and reporters yelled, "Tess, over here!" Dick and I fought our way through the crowd into the lobby of the hotel, where I was checked in and escorted to my room.

When I finally got inside and closed the door with a sigh, I saw Skinner standing in the center of the room.

I got very still. He did not advance, but kept his distance. "Tessa, I know we didn't part the best of friends last time. And I'm sorry about that bruise on your thigh. ("At least it didn't show," he thought to himself with pride. He had learned how to hit a woman so no one would notice, especially in church.) "Look, Tess, I want to make peace with you. Just have your picture taken with me—that's all I ask. I am in line for a really big Las Vegas reality show and am looking for sponsors. Your endorsement would be a great draw. It won't cost you anything. In fact, I will pay you. Just name your price."

"You already know the price, Skinner. Jess paid it a long time ago," I said. He just stood there, with his beer belly and goatee, half a shirt tail hanging out. He was sweating profusely. "What happened to the priest's robe?" I asked.

"Oh, they found me out and de-frocked me. Some cleaning lady ratted me out. But I am still a member in good standing until the paperwork comes through. With that group it could be three, maybe four hundred years. I still have my hand in the pie, so to speak."

"And this current getup?" I asked.

"Why Tess, don't you recognize a televangelist when you see one? Amen Hallelujah! The Devil is out to get you! Send money and pass the offering plate!"

"The Devil talking about the Devil. That IS a clever disguise," I said, walking over to get a bottle of water, suddenly very thirsty.

"Works every time," he said. "You see, talking about the Devil stirs up fear and hatred, and those are my two best friends! Listen to this: 'Thank you, sister for the cookies and the cakes and the taking care of the children. Pass your money along and keep showing up, but you be sure to stay in the back now, hear? You ladies know your place.' How do I sound?"

"Sadly enough, you fit right in," I said.

"I've been working on the accent," Skinner said

"Tess, you're not being reasonable. These people aren't worth saving. Look how they treated your brother. Look how they are treating you. Has even one person stepped up to be your friend? They don't even know who you are. At least I know who you are. We have memories in common, Contessa. A common homeland."

"That's enough, Skinner. I know who you really are. And soon they will too."

"We'll see, Tessa. They don't search very deeply, as you know."

He came closer to me, licking his lips as he looked me up and down. "Please, please endorse me. It will only be for a little while... Imagine how beautiful you could be if seen alongside me, especially with no clothes on. We could shoot the video right here."

"True beauty has nothing to do with bodies, Skinner. You know that. We don't even need them at the Ranch. So why do you get people to focus so much energy on things like looks, and sex, and gender?"

"Don't you get it, Contessa? When they are thinking about their bodies, they won't be thinking about their souls! Besides," he said, continuing, "doesn't it say somewhere in Scripture, go and preach to all the genitals?"

"It says 'Gentiles,' Skinner. You know that."

"Ah, but with that other interpretation I have had so much fun! I've gotten people bound up for years, even killed over that one."

I took a breath and then said, "That's it. I'm done with you."

As I turned away I added, "Go ahead and show yourself to the door, Skinner. Crawl out if you need to."

"You are done with me?" he yelled. "Not by a long shot, Miss Apple of your Father's Eye. It is you who will be finished tomorrow!" he said, slamming the door. In the hallway, he passed Dick as he stood outside the door. "Do it," he snarled, never making eye contact.

I called Solomon's number, which Dick had given me in the car ride over to the hotel. But it went straight to voice mail, which said: "Sorry I can't take your call right now. I am in meetings with very important people, helping them attain their dreams and financial goals. For more information, press 1. To place your stock order, press 2. For media requests, press 3."

I pressed "3," and then left a voice mail with an assistant named "Bambi:" "Solomon, I am here for you. Please meet with me again. Tess."

I stayed in my room the next day, but my phone never rang. To make things even worse, it seems "they" had misplaced Joshua at the airport. His crate had somehow come open on the tarmac and the airlines were "very sorry… they were doing all they could, were hopeful that he would be found, etc. etc."

I threw my head back against the headboard when I heard the news. "Joshua, please find your way back to me," was all that I could say. The difference between dogs and humans, I was beginning to realize, is that dogs keep searching until they find you.

Right before I drifted off to sleep, I remembered how one of Dad's favorite games on the Ranch was hide and seek. He would hide behind a rock or a cloud, and then Jess and I would search for him.

We would look for clues. "Daddy, are you in the wind?" Hearing no answer, we would ask, "Are you in the storm?" Again, no answer. Jess would go knock on every door at the Ranch, asking, "Are you in there?" until finally Dad would leap out and say "I AM!" We would then jump all over him and he would laugh. One thing I've got to say for Jess—he would knock and knock and never give up. Jess knew the meaning of persistence, that is for sure.

Just then there was a knock at my door. Hoping someone had found Joshua, or even that it might be Solomon, come to me at last, I got up and opened it. The door swung open and a very large, red-faced, out-of-breath man flashed a badge and said:

"Contessa Some Foreign Name I Can't Pronounce," he said. "You are under arrest for very suspicious activity. You have the right to remain silent. Anything you do or say can and will be used against you in a court of law. You have the right to an attorney..." he continued with what I knew were my Miranda rights. "Do you have anything to say for yourself?" he asked, as he clicked on the handcuffs.

"This is just great," I said, and meant it. If Solomon didn't have time for me when he was flying high, I would just have to meet him at the bottom when he fell. I had begun to realize that somehow getting him to listen to me was the fastest way to bring us all home.

Headlines the next day read: "Mystery Genius Charged: NSA Cites Untraceable Bank Deposits as Crime."

It didn't matter what the headlines read. I knew my honor was written in stone, and was not subject to the daily news. I also knew the charges had been trumped up. Dick and Judith had no doubt forged my name to all sorts of documents behind my back. So the "evidence" was of course all there. A large amount of money with no traceable source had become a very serious government offense. Dick and Judith turned state's witness at the trial, and said they were shocked when they discovered that I wasn't who I said I was.

I was three days in a holding cell, and on the final day I knew what was coming. The jury found me guilty. I was sentenced to the Pit.

▪ ▪ ▪

Fia knew what it was to be in a Pit. When the news came back that her brother Nissi was dead, she had tumbled into a pit of her own—of grief, of blame, of guilt. Why hadn't she been there to save him? Why did he have to die instead of her? The questions and anger had turned into a cloud of despair, one she couldn't cope with. In fact, she had simply stopped speaking after Nissi's funeral. Her parents had tried everything to lift her spirits—they had even suggested hiking as a way to get her mind off the past. "How ironic," Fia thought. "Here I am in a Pit, and now so is Contessa."

▪ ▪ ▪

Part Three:

THE PIT

Chapter Twenty-Four

The Pit was a place Skinner himself controlled. He had taken over an abandoned gravel pit and had secured the "rehabilitation" contract under one of his many enterprises. He had convinced the authorities that he could take care of things. "Just turn them all over to me," he had said. "I'll take them off your hands."

The country's criminal system had become so expensive that they didn't use bars anymore to keep people in. They just distilled and bottled the scent of human fear. All Skinner did was pipe that scent in massive sporadic blasts around the perimeter. It kept everyone in, and out. The guard tower he set up was just a ruse—an illusion for the authorities. He knew he had ways to keep even the innocent trapped, if they let him. Since the state's Governor named Mai Apathy had signed the contract without even reading it, Skinner had pretty much free reign.

After the criminals were sentenced, they were loaded into cattle trucks and driven to the very edge of the massive Pit. Then the back door was opened, and each of us, one at a time, was shoved over the edge.

Even knowing the ending of something doesn't keep it from hurting. So it still felt horrible when I was tossed like garbage over the side.

Once again I found myself falling, and landing with a thud.

I must have blacked out for a moment, because when I came to I thought I must be having a very bad dream.

There he was, wearing tight black leather pants, a vest, and a tattoo that read "I've Lost my Way" with a big gash through it. He held a whip in one hand and a pitchfork in the other. I couldn't help but start laughing when I saw his latest getup. I blinked several times to realize that this was not a dream. I saw him approach with his unique way of walking that can only be called The Slide.

"Really, Skinner, such a cliché. A pitchfork? You never worked with a pitchfork a day in your life!"

"Shut up, Contessa," Skinner snarled. "You're in my territory now. You will do what I tell you to do. I am the boss."

"Not exactly," said a voice, stepping out from the shadows. I looked up to see Solomon, wearing his gold calf ring.

"Oh," said Skinner, quickly changing his tone. "Sully. How nice to see you! And what brought you here to this fine Pit, may I ask?"

"Derivatives," Sully said quietly.

He turned in my direction, and I was shocked to realize he was blind in one eye. "I think I recognize the sound of your voice. Who are you?" he asked.

Skinner jumped in and said, "Sully, she's a nobody. Don't waste your time on women, remember? They only lead to trouble. Come on now, let's talk about an idea I have for you on how to run things around here." Seeing how easily Solomon was still swayed by Skinner, I decided on a different plan. Revealing myself before he was ready to really see me, and hear me, would not accomplish what I wanted. I needed to work with the others first.

I made my way over to the crowd and saw Skinner standing on a stack of garbage. People were forced to line up in front of him and repeat: "I am Illegal, Oppressed, and Unwanted." He then had them each sign a giant declaration page that read simply, I.O.U. After each day's signatures were gathered he posted it by the entrance.

They were then given their "Orientation Kits." Each kit contained a large dried manure chip which was to be "placed immediately upon the shoulder."

Skinner had obviously figured out that guarding a chip on one's shoulder would cause the person's neck to become stiff and unable to turn quickly. He once said he hated how Jess and I always walked so straight forward, easily looking left or right, able to respond to Mom or Dad's calling from any direction. I sensed immediately that his aim with these "manure chips" was also to cause people to lose proper alignment. This would increase stress in every major muscle group and cause them to start walking "naturally" in crooked ways. When the head was down guarding a chip the person would also begin to move in smaller and smaller circles in order to avoid contact with others. Eventually, if Skinner's plan worked, "chip guarders" would sooner or later be standing in some corner, alone.

Also inside the kit were blank labels as well as several large stones. Each person received unlimited prescription "tab loids," which were to be placed under the tongue. The effect, Skinner knew, would be to get the tongue to let loose and start wagging. The "tab loids" also caused the tongue to secrete a special acid, which would inevitably spew forth in dialogue, dissolving anything or anyone it touched.

Skinner explained the program in the Pit like this:

"Place and then guard the large chip on your shoulder. Each chip was selectively hand-picked for you based on your past. Some of these chips even go back for generations. Each one of them has been freeze dried in the freezer called Revenge. Do not let your chips fall off, no matter what. The longer you are able to keep them on your shoulder, the sooner the chips will melt and flow organically down your torso. This melting will further enable the manure scent to mingle with your own, creating a very distinctive *odeur* indeed."

"You are also to take these blank labels that have been provided and label everyone around you as quickly as possible. One or two word labels will do, especially if based on outward appearances such as race, size, age, or gender. In fact, the shorter the label, the better. If you cannot immediately place the label on their chest, their forehead will do.

Stone throwing is allowed and encouraged. You may hurl stones at will, for any reason, at any time."

This program was designed to create nothing but chaos, confusion, and disharmony. Some began brushing up against others for the sheer purpose of knocking their chips off. Fights broke out with manure chips flying everywhere. When labels were applied it became obvious that even "families" couldn't get along. "You Liberal!" one would shout. "Coward," another would yell, while another would spit out "Pig!" There seemed to be no shortage of one-word labels to apply to others.

I couldn't help but wonder what all that energy would be like if it were harnessed and applied elsewhere.

▪ ▪ ▪

When I woke up that next morning it was not to the smell of coffee. It was to the smell of burning rubber. I also heard a chorus that sounded like groaning and moaning. Remembering my lessons from the forest, I went to the center of the square, sat myself down in the dust, and listened. What was really going on? What was underneath the sounds? What was prompting them?

Underneath it all was an undertow made of two constant sounds. I tilted my head and then it came to me. The entire noise rising out of the pit was based on two words. One was "Me." Which was repeated sometime in staccato fashion: "Me! Me! Me!" and then about every third measure, it was attached to the second word: "Want."

"ME WANT! ME WANT! ME WANT!" was the constant tone I heard.

How could these people be so self-centered and out of balance as a result? I would definitely have to work on this.

I decided to go over to a place Skinner's orientation map called "The Recreation Center." However, nobody seemed to be having a good time despite the very high activity level. I quickly renamed it "Blamer's Lodge." It was full of people with broken fingers. It seemed they had one digit on either hand that was permanently immovable, fixed in a gesture pointing at someone else. This seemed to render all their other fingers inoperable.

This group spent the entire day pointing at others outside the center yelling, "There goes the cause of all my trouble." One man stood there with a drink in his hand. "That woman over there—she's the one that caused me to drink," he growled as he threw back another swig.

A woman on a bar stool pointed to a man walking past. "He's the one who made me leave my husband. I was such a nice girl before I met him."

Around "happy hour," they would all gather around and start pointing to everyone gathered outside their lodge. Now entire groups were the cause of their trouble. Skinner just kept serving at the bar, smiling the whole time.

As I surveyed this group I thought to myself, "Mom wouldn't stand for this one minute."

I remembered that Mom always said that an artistic approach could solve many a tangled situation. I went to the graffiti supply warehouse, which was open 24/7, and grabbed a couple of cans of silver metallic paint.

I took them to the Blamer's Lodge, and I started at the bottom of the window and began to spray, evenly, gently, constantly, left to right, then right to left on the return. (Mom had taught me that consistency in application is the key to all success.)

At first they didn't notice me. People there were so busy pointing at others outside the glass. Soon my activity stopped them. I had turned their window into a giant reflective mirror.

One by one, their hands dropped to their sides as they realized the finger they were pointing at others was now firmly pointing back at them. People began to stumble out of the once so comfortable Lodge. They now stood in silence without a word to say.

Slowly, they made their way back to their hovels, some of them still murmuring, "My life could have been so much better if only..."

Primero and Ultima had set up camp in a far corner of the Pit. They told me they had been deported shortly after I left them the note and had landed here. "We tried to convince them that we were legal, but they refused to honor our papers, saying a land grant four centuries years old did not entitle us to citizenship."

They had an idea and asked if I would help them secretly. I readily agreed, and every evening after that I was with them, helping them with their project.

I had observed a different group, which met in a hall of mirrors. On the map it was called "Your Beauty Spa," but to me it became known as Poser's Palace. The entire interior walls were painted with reflective silver paint so that those within it could admire themselves from every angle. They studied themselves up close, far away, from behind, and from side to side. Occasionally, Skinner would walk in and make a remark to one of them like, "Wow, your nose sure is big" or "Those lips are looking a little thin." This created a flurry of upset. People began trying to swap body parts. This person wanted that person's nose, and this person wanted so-and-so's torso. There was much flexing and strutting, posing, comparing, and gnashing of teeth.

I left the Palace and went to Skinner's tool shed. He had so many scraping and cutting instruments that it took me twenty minutes to decide which one to use. Finally, I made my decision.

I returned to the entrance of Poser's Palace and slowly, steadily I began to scrape the silver off of the back of the mirrors.

Nobody noticed me for hours. There was always another reflective surface to turn to. When I had gotten nearly all the silver backing scraped off, I was amazed to see some of the people admiring their reflection in the sunglasses of someone standing next to them. “This is ridiculous,” I thought.

Soon, however, they were all standing there having to look beyond themselves. There were no more mirrors. All that remained were windows looking out on a pit full of misery and suffering. The people began to walk back to their cells one by one, hanging their heads down low. I overheard one of them ask, “If I can’t see my reflection, what reason is there to live?”

▪ ▪ ▪

The next morning Skinner pushed his cart into the center of the square. He carefully unfolded the pop-up banners that told of his wares. He congratulated himself again for allowing prisoners to bring cash and debit cards with them to the Pit. Those that didn't have any, he loaned some, with significant interest, shall we say.

It was one of his better business decisions, he chuckled to himself, along with allowing an open bar.

He plunged the holder into the dirt, laid out his chains and necklaces on each side, and then put four or five of them around his neck, waiting for people to arrive.

"What do I do with this?" asked one woman, picking up a cross necklace.

"Point it at your boyfriend, and the vampire will go away!" he laughed.

Next came a teenaged girl. "What about me?" she asked.

"Oh, darling, there is nothing like a cross for a fashion statement. Look here. I have them in gold, silver, platinum."

"I heard they have magical powers," said a teenaged boy.

"Oh, they do, but only the very, very, very expensive ones. If you buy this one and get all your friends to buy one too, it will help you get that violent game you've been wanting."

Sales were brisk. He loved selling crosses. He dealt in other items, of course, most profitably diamonds, but he loved selling crosses on the weekend. It allowed him to mingle with the people.

A couple stepped out of the shadows. "How much for that one?" they asked, pointing to the large wooden one, which held all the others. "Oh, that one is not for sale. You wouldn't want it anyway. Look, it's made of old scratchy wood. It still has thorns stuck in it. I think there might even be blood stains here and there. This is for display only. I use it to sell the good ones, the new ones, the shiny ones," he said, trying to distract their gaze.

"We want it," said the couple firmly. "We'll pay whatever you ask."

Skinner smiled, knowing this demand usually sent others scurrying. "You can have it for free. Just know that when you pick it up, you will probably bleed," he said.

"Done," said the man. He and the woman walked over to the stand, carefully removing the smaller crosses of silver and gold. As the man worked to free the heavy base, one of the thorns cut his hand. As small blood drops began to run down his wrist, the woman came over and helped him. Soon she too had hands full of scrapes and splinters. Yet they worked on. Skinner stood silently, shaking his head as the man and woman then lifted the heavy worthless wooden beams and dragged them away.

"You meet the strangest people here," Skinner said to himself. "I should have stayed in Vegas."

For some reason he lost his taste for selling that day—for the rest of the day anyway. Skinner counted and then pocketed his change, gathered up the remaining shiny crosses, and headed off into the darkness.

▪ ▪ ▪

Chapter Twenty-Five

One of my favorite memories on the Ranch was when we would all get our lawn chairs and head down to sit by the Gate. There was a young shepherd boy named David who loved to sing when he watched the sheep, and his songs wafted up to us with the most beautiful chords. Dad said, "Well, at least one Valley Lander can sing." Mom agreed. We were all really taken by the lyrics to his songs. They all were really songs of longing for us. These concerts by King David, as he later became known, were one of our favorite Friday night events.

Thinking that one way to create harmony would be to get these Valley Landers singing, I put up a hand-lettered sign. "Choir practice. Tomorrow night. 7:30." We would see if anyone showed up.

Choir practice was disheartening, even for me. Of the six people who showed up, four were tone deaf from listening to loud music. One fancied herself an opera star and kept prancing out to the center of the group, telling the others to shut up so we could all hear her. We could hear her, all right.

Even I reached for earplugs that night. The other person who showed up said he could only sing if the words mother, truck, or beer were in the lyrics. Another young man jumped up and began to speak loud, fast rhyming words while grabbing his crotch every third verse. This would surely not do.

After surveying the situation, I ascertained that a better use of our time would be a humming class. Humming is always better than whining, Mom used to say, and there was enough whining going on here to last a lifetime.

"Everyone can hum," I thought. And so the class began. I had them all sit up straight and tap their chest with the four fingers of their right hand. "Your heart is here. Now make a sound that causes your chest bone to resonate." At first there were highs and lows, and I thought someone named Squeaky might have joined us, but soon everyone found their sound. It was amazing.

"There are two new sounds we are going to learn to hum together," I said. "'We' is the first one. As you say it, and look around at your neighbors, realize you are not alone.

They did this dutifully, beginning to sound, "We… We… We…"

"The second word," I said, "is 'have.' Say it slowly. Consider all the resources we have here together as a group." Slowly, the group began to chant the words I had taught them.

"We Have…." exhale "We Have…" inhale… "We have…" exhale. The energy shifted in the room and people began to relax.

Apparently, some people at the monster truck rally even heard it and came by the next morning for class. Soon, the original six had grown to 22. From 22 people it grew to 100. The background noise now coming from the place was not Me Me Me Want Want Want anymore, but just the opposite.

It was a lovely sound. "We..." said slowly and full of grace. "Have." So calming, so abundant, so full. Inhale "we." Exhale "have."

People began to smile at one another as they breathed the words together.

The Pit began to experience its first semblance of Peace.

▪ ▪ ▪

Meanwhile, however, Solomon and Skinner had sectioned off a part of the Pit as their own. Solomon was attempting to escape it, an effort I found ironic since Skinner, his so-called partner in the venture, was also the one who ran the whole enterprise. However, knowing what a liar Skinner was, and how easily he tricked people into thinking he was working with them to reach their goals, it didn't surprise me that Solomon was so ensnared.

If he could keep "Sully," as he called him, busy even with this escape plan, Sully would not have time to seek me out.

Skinner had designed a "rock-climbing escape route," where he would supposedly help people get a jump out of the Pit.

He and Sully would take their money and then offer them various routes. One was called "Let's Get High," and before they began their climb they were given a drug so powerful it made them vomit and fall down before they even took the first step up.

The other program was called "Corporate Ladders." People, some still wearing their business suits, tried to get ahead, often by stepping on the person ahead of them. In one particular contest I observed, several of them even held others down, thinking this would help them get ahead faster.

Their climb was short lived. What greeted them "at the top" was the realization that their ladders were perched against a wall that went nowhere. Skinner had other routes, too, some involving sleazy dancers and one called "Cleavage Maximus." I noticed lots of women and men signing up for that one. I guess they were attracted by the loud pulsing beat and the fact that Skinner had installed a tall silver pole. But when the women tried to climb up it, they just slid down and around it slowly. (Evidently this was the plan, as then the men forgot about escape altogether and would pay for more dancing.)

Sully surveyed all of this, collecting fees, telling people where to go, which line to stand in, making recommendations. However, I could tell he was losing his enthusiasm for these endeavors.

But he still didn't ask for me. I overhead him say one day, "I can figure this out on my own."

▪ ▪ ▪

Skinner walked up beside me as I took my morning walk, picking up trash and plastic bottles and putting them in a bag I carried for that purpose.

"He can't really hear you anymore, you know. He lost some of his hearing in the mining accident."

I said nothing, but just kept walking.

"It was really his fault, not mine. He kept wanting bigger drill bits and bigger drill bits, which of course make more noise. I think he lost his hearing gradually, never knowing it was going. Of course, the gold and diamond dust that I put in his ears every night certainly helped things along," Skinner said.

"He still has vision in one eye, though. When the blasting caps at the diamond mine went off, I thought I had maneuvered him close enough so it would blind him altogether. Someone, I don't know who, called his name at the last minute, and he turned away."

"That was me," I said. "Solomon did hear me then. And he will hear me again."

"The Valley Landers aren't all dumb, Skinner," I said. "Some of them will figure you out."

"Oh really," he said, laying down his pitchfork. "This thing is heavy! No wonder I never worked with it. But back to the topic at hand.... If 'Soul of Mine' as you call him is so smart, then why did your beloved sell me his senses in exchange for the ring?"

I said nothing, not wanting to continue a conversation with a fool.

"To be honest, it took awhile," he continued, now just talking to hear himself. "At first all he wanted was to spend time with you. 'I have to go see her, he would say. She is all I desire!'" Skinner said in a mocking voice.

"If you were going to meet him at eight, I would try to distract him at seven. I just did little things at first. I stole his pen one day, so he couldn't write you. I noticed he didn't make the effort to find another one."

"In a particular stroke of genius, I had the Queen of Sheba come and fawn all over him. She brought him so many presents it took days to count them. He began to believe what everyone was saying, that he was the wisest of them all. I knew then that I had him. Pride goeth before a fall, as somebody once wrote somewhere. Anyway. It doesn't matter."

Skinner continued his dialogue, enjoying immensely the retelling of his seduction. "One day, I took him out to the edge of town and said, "Sully, if you listen to me, I will make sure your bank accounts are never empty! We will build skyscrapers with your name on them. Because one can never have enough monuments, right? Slowly, he believed me. And when I told him this ring would help him rule forever, well, he just fell for it. It didn't happen overnight. But, as you can see, he wears it constantly now."

I remembered it well—the ring with the bull's head and fiery eyes, turned into a seal of "authority and power."

"Skinner," I said to him. "You are the king of dust."

▪ ▪ ▪

Often at night I would go and sit with little "huerfana," an orphan who cried herself to sleep. I would hold and rock her. After she fell asleep I would gather her tears in a little cup, and slip over to Solomon's quarters. I would tip the cup so that the little girl's tears would drop one at a time into his ears. Perhaps the tears could dissolve the gold that Skinner had been pouring into his ears all these years. It was worth a try.

▪ ▪ ▪

Chapter Twenty-Six

I walked beside Solomon every day, slightly to the left and behind him. For many reasons, I suppose, not just the reasons Skinner gave, he could not see or hear me. His eyes, once wide with wonder, now seemed like slits of anger. I remembered that I used to be able to hear him humming as he came up the hill to meet me. Now all I heard were grunts of dissatisfaction and orders barked out across the yard. "Do this now!" he would say. "Because I said so!" he would bellow and then threaten to cuff the offending party with the back of his hand. I observed the two of them working together like this. Skinner convinced Sully to single out anyone who looked weak, small, or frail and cast them aside. "Let them fend for themselves," Skinner would say.

Then, he had Solomon single out the strongest men and demand that they try to lift him up. His attempts to force people to help him up were going nowhere, as at best, with forced labor, he could only get as high as two people.

Meanwhile, he had developed a rival named HuSez. HuSez was determined to prove Sully wrong and would challenge him at every turn. He refused to help Sully scale the wall and instead often tried to trip him when he was walking. Or he would bribe one of the "carriers" to suddenly collapse.

I decided not to interfere in this folly but concentrate instead on the people who wanted to learn.

I began having early morning classes, and people began to attend.

One lesson was the singing bowl. (I had learned this one from Mom.) I gave them each a silver bowl and asked them to rub their fingers around the inside of it, slow and steady, slow and steady, concentrating on the motion of their hands.

Soon, an amazing series of sounds arose from the group. It was full and rich and held promise and beauty and life. One man named Tiny with two missing teeth began to let tears flow down his face. "This is so beautiful," he said. "I wish my mama were alive."

The next day I told them to bring their bowls to class full of water. All of them brought lukewarm water that tasted terrible. I remembered when Skinner once gave Jess a cup of water when he was in the field. Jess took a sip of it and then spewed it out, saying, "Skinner, give it to me hot, or give it to me cold. This lukewarm stuff of yours tastes like spit!"

I told the group I had some new liquid I wanted to share. I went around to each one but could not share my new drink with them because their bowls were full.

"If you want to make room for something new, you have to get rid of what is old." (I had learned a variation of this lesson with Jess. We had used wineskins and gotten in a lot of trouble when Dad found out. Maybe it was because we took it upon ourselves to make room for the new wine by drinking the old wine. We did extra barn cleaning time for that little lesson, let me tell you.)

But I was older now, using water instead of wine, and the people more and more seemed grateful and eager to learn.

Yet the rivalry between Sully and HuSez continued. It seemed to usually involve discussions of parentage and territory. The constant battled seemed to be who was entitled to which section of dirt. One day their conflict erupted beyond words. Sully said "This area is mine." HuSez yelled back, "No, it's mine!"

And then it began. Each man thrust his head forward in challenge. One shoulder brushed up against the other. Then someone's hand came up and shoved. Then there was a punch to the gut and a wild swing at a jaw and suddenly there was a conflagration of shouting and twisting, writhing bodies trying to pummel each other into submission. Submission to what? To whom? It didn't matter, really. A fight was a fight, and both knew they were in this one to win.

The crowd that usually gathered around fights did so again, except this time, instead of yelling and encouraging the violence, they joined hands, and began to hum. Softly at first, and then with increasing volume.

Sully lunged at HuSez again and knocked him to the ground. HuSez struggled to get up, but Sully flipped him over and then emerged on top. He pinned his arms down on the ground with his knees, and he reached over and found a rock. He raised it high up over his head and was clearly about to destroy the man beneath him. The group's humming sound was now so loud it was causing the very ground to vibrate.

I shouted, "Solomon!"

He turned his head slightly to the sound of my voice, still grasping the rock in his hand.

"Solomon," I said again, drawing closer to him.

"Contessa, is that you?" he asked, a look of confusion replacing the anger on his face.

"Yes, it's me." I paused. "The question is—Solomon, is this you?"

He looked toward me, and then around at the circle, and then down at the vanquished foe beneath him. But this time he did not see the face of his enemy anymore. He saw only his own image superimposed over the man he was about to destroy.

Suddenly realizing that he was about to kill, really, himself, he dropped the rock. It landed in a large rain puddle beside them and caused a ripple that made a familiar sound.

I remembered then that this was the vision I had seen, so many years ago out at Crystal Lake.

He slowly stood, put his arm out, and pulled up HuSez. "I am sorry," Solomon said. "I didn't really see who you were. I didn't really see me."

When he did this I moved even closer toward him, on the side of his "good eye." He then reached out to embrace me and began kissing my ears, my neck, my mouth. "Why didn't you make yourself known to me?" Solomon asked, when he stopped to get his breath.

"I have been trying for years. You were too busy and then too distracted."

"Forgive me, Contessa. You were all I ever wanted."

"What about the Queen of Sheba?" I couldn't help but ask. "I heard from the Ranch Hands and Skinner you wanted her pretty badly too. "

"Oh, she left me early on. Went on to bigger and better things. They were all nothing, meant nothing, I can see that now. Contessa, talk to me. Sing to me. Let me hear your voice! I have missed the sound of you." He added softly, "As you can see, I haven't done very well on my own."

I said, "There is only one way out of this Pit, Solomon, and if everybody listens I will show you all how." The people gathered around me, and I began to speak.

"Solomon, you and HuSez—you are the strongest. Kneel down together shoulder to shoulder, side by side. Next, you two over there, the next strongest—kneel shoulder to shoulder beside them." I then directed the next strongest to form a second layer resting on their shoulders. They then were told to reach out to the next strongest among them and help them climb on top of them. This went on until we had a human pyramid, based with the strongest at the bottom, allowing those with less strength to rest on top of them. At last we were down to the little girl who stood crying off to the side.

Solomon asked, "Who is that?"

"She calls herself Huerfana," I told him.

He said, "Doesn't that mean orphan?"

"That is what she is," I said.

"Not anymore," he said, calling out to her. "Step up, Beloved, you can do it." His hand reached out to lift her up, and at each level she was met with other hands. Finally she was at the very top of the Pit.

I told her, "Stretch out your hand as far as it will go, holding the present I gave you." And suddenly I saw it. My father's outstretched hand. Just like Michaelangelo had painted it in the

Sistine Chapel. Instead this time Dad was not sending someone away but was reaching out to bring everyone home.

When the little girl's fingers touched Dad's, a blazing sun broke out as he smiled and held up the present for all to see. It was the mustard seed Jess had given me when he left the Ranch. Suddenly everyone was shouting and trumpets blared.

At first, all we all could see were Dad and Mom standing there, holding the little girl. They weren't high above us anymore, but we were all now on the same level. Behind them rose a booming, opalescent cloud.

Jess stepped out from the cloud. He emerged slowly, with both arms hidden behind him. "I brought something for you, Contessa."

I looked up and saw him leading Verdad, with Espiritu prancing at his side. "I told you someday they would show up at the same place, at the same time. Truth and Spirit, together at last."

"Well done, Contessa," said Dad. "You have finished the work your brother started."

"Just like he said you would," beamed Mom.

Chattanango walked up leading another animal, and pointed to Solomon. "Here. This one's for you." We all laughed when we saw that it was a mule who was balking and refusing to be led.

Just then, I noticed two people making their way through the crowd. It was Primero and Ultima, and they were holding something in their hands. Everyone turned to see an incredibly beautiful vine, blossoming from a piece of the old, unwanted cross they had taken away from Skinner.

"We took this, and planted it. We watered it and tended it every day, sending it our love and prayers and sadness, and this is the fruit we have." They both stepped forward and faced Mom and Dad. "Once, you made a Garden for us. Now we have made a Garden for you." And they handed them the basket of fruits they had grown. Jess then walked over and picked up the giant IOU contract everyone had signed that was permanently posted at the entrance to the pit. "This debt has been paid in full," he declared, tearing it in half.

Skinner stood nearby. He began to clap—one loud clap. "I am so touched by all of this, I think I'm going to cry," he said. "NOT!" he yelled sarcastically and tried to grab Ultima.

Chattanango's voice called out, "Now?"

"Now," Dad replied.

Chattanango then took the chain Skinner had forged for every slave ever bought or sold. With a snap of his wrist Chattanango curled it around Skinner's feet, and, in an instant, Skinner was on the ground, Chattanango standing over him.

"Hand me the vessel, Q," he said, "the one that you designed."

Q handed him a long silver tube. Chattanango looked over at me and winked, pointing to the engraving that read "Custom Designed by Quo Vadis. Triple A Approved."

As Chattanango stood confronting Skinner, all of us gathered around. We saw the former Pit boss begin to shrink in size. His face, arms and feet simply diminished. Right before us, the once magnificent, then fallen and feared, source of lies and sorrow became a wormish thing. "I've been waiting to do this a thousand years," said Chattanango. He picked up Skinner, who was now no bigger than the S on this page, and dropped him into the vessel Q had designed. He then grabbed the tube and whirled in a tight, small circle. On his third turn he released it and hurled the tube out into solar space. We all stood silently and watched as, far, far away it finally disappeared, shattering into millions of mirrored shards.

Solomon turned to Chattanango, refusing to take the mule. He said, "Thanks, but if you don't mind I think I will be riding with her from now on." He walked over to Espiritu, grabbed her mane, and swung up right behind me. "I'm never going to let anything come between us again, my Love," he said, nuzzling my neck. "Will you marry me?" With that, he took off the ring he had been wearing and offered it to me.

"That ring represents a bunch of bull, you do realize that now, don't you?" I said. "Look at its horns, fiery eyes, and stuck-out tongue. That is ugly!"

"Yes," he said, "but it's all I have to give you."

"Drop it," I said gently. "I already have a ring. Just give me your empty hand. Solomon, all I ever wanted was to be with you in a simple circle of love, because that is all I have ever known. And as for marriage," I added, "well, let's take that one day at a time. You're way behind on your homework."

Dad walked up and said, "Did somebody say marriage? This calls for a celebration!"

To our astonishment, even HuSez agreed.

Dad and Mom took it all in. They saw Primero and Ultima hugging Jess, presenting him the very fine grapes they had grown. They saw people crowded around in joy, lifting up little Huerfana. Isaiah brought in an oxcart and handed out garlands in exchange for ashes and joy for their tears. Ezekiel stood nearby, greeting old bones he recognized. Elijah threw his arm around the widow, saying something that made her laugh.

They saw Solomon embracing me with all his might, his lips pressed closely against my ear. Seeing everyone gathered around looking so happy, I shouted out, "Ok, everybody, let's go home!"

Mom and Dad turned to me with a smile and said, "Contessa, we are home."

Chattanango raised the hammer called Justice and let it fall again and again, shattering all the walls of the Pit. Righteousness and Peace began to roll down before us in a shimmering cascade of Light... like a waterfall.

■ ■ ■

The pages of the journal went blank.

Fia scanned the rest of the book, looking for more writing but instead found only blank pages.

"I wonder what that means," she thought as she turned to stand. Still feeling slightly off balance, she grabbed a rock to catch herself. When she did her hand fell on the final page. Gathering the journal closer, she saw that what she thought was just an ink smudge was really a fingerprint. Right beside it was the newly made imprint of dust from her thumb, too. Her eyes grew wide in the gathering light as she realized the two fingerprints were the same.

In the distance she could hear Joshua barking. She could also hear her mother and father calling out, "Sophia! Beloved! Where are you?"

Suddenly, she heard Nissi's voice whispering in her ear, "Sophia, the whole world is searching for you. Are you ready?"

In a Voice no longer still, no longer small, she called out, "I Am!" and stepped through the waterfall.

▪ ▪ ▪

With Special Thanks to:

Shelly Shepherd, whose undying devotion has helped make all of this come true

Studio G, for the many early readings and encouragement

The Path Community, who have heard this story for years in snippets and sections around campfires, in board rooms, and during very long weekends

My family, especially my sister Kathy and my brother Joe, who made growing up so much fun, and were the inspiration for many of the happy scenes on the Ranch

Catherine C. Calhoun, who has believed in Contessa from day one

Rev. Karen Clark Ristine, for editing and encouragement

Sonya Steckler, for final copy edits and enthusiasm

For more information about The Contessa Chronicles, or other works by Laurie Beth Jones please contact:

888 525 7371 Ext 3 (phone)
www.lauriebethjones.com (website)
info@lauriebethjones.com (email)
twitter: @LaurieBethJones
LBJ: Inspiring Divine Connection

Scripture References

and Imagery used as touch points for The Contessa Chronicles: A Sampling

Wisdom there in the beginning—Proverbs 8: 22-31

Let us make man in "our" image—Genesis 1:26

Adam and Eve: The fall—Genesis 3: 1-24

Jess sent to learn a trade—Mark 6:3, Matthew 13:55

God in the garden—Genesis 2:8

Satan falls from heaven—Isaiah 14:12, Luke 10:18

King David singing Psalms—Psalms 1-150

God: A thousand years is like a day—Psalms 90:4, 2 Peter 3:8

Song of Deborah—Judges 5

Trumpets of Jericho—Joshua 6: 1-27

Elijah and the chariots—2 Kings 2:11

Elijah and the robe—2 Kings 2:13

Elijah revives a dying boy—1 Kings 17: 17-23

Holy Spirit leads/drives Jesus into Wilderness—Mark 1:12

Blaspheming the Holy Spirit the only unforgivable sin—
Mark 3: 28-29

Jesus refers to Elijah and John the Baptist—Matthew 11:14

The Flood—Genesis 6-9

Jesus talks to woman at the well—John 4: 5-42

Jesus in the midst of a crowd—Matthew 18:20

Holy Spirit falls from heaven—Acts 2:1-4

Solomon asks for wisdom—1 Kings 3:16-28

Book of Proverbs

Book of Ecclesiastes

Song of Songs

River Scene in Prophets Tour: Ezekiel 47

Valley of dry bones: Ezekiel 37

Solomon builds the temple: 1 Kings 6

Solomon builds his own house: 1 Kings 7

Solomon and the Queen of Sheba—1 Kings 10: 1-13

Spirit of God fills the temple at completion—2 Chronicles 7:1

Lions lying down with the lambs—Isaiah 11:6

Everyone sitting under his own fig tree—Micah 4:4

Old wine into new wineskins—Luke 5: 33-39

Jesus crucifixion—Mark 15: 16-39

Lessons in the Pit: Broad Themes

Accountability—Romans 14:12

The Bride must make herself ready—Revelation 19:7

Compassion—Matthew 25: 31-46

Pure religion is to take care of orphans—James 1:27

Truth and Spirit come together—John 4:24

Satan is banished—Isaiah 14: 12-13, Revelations 20:1

Heavenly reunion—Revelations Chapter 21

Joyous Reunion—Isaiah 60

Invitation—Revelations 22:17

Wisdom

Wisdom is radiant and unfading, and she is easily discerned by those who love her, and is found by those who seek her. She hastens to make herself known to those who desire her. One who rises early to seek her will have no difficulty, for she will be found sitting at the gate. To fix one's thought on her is perfect understanding, and one who is vigilant on her account will soon be free from care, because she goes about seeking those worthy of her, and she graciously appears to them in their paths, and meets them in every thought.

Wisdom of Solomon 6:12-16 From the New Revised Standard Version (Anglicized Edition) of the Bible

Other Books
by Laurie Beth Jones

Jesus, CEO: Using Ancient Wisdom for Visionary Leadership

The Path: Creating Your Mission for Work and Life

The Path for Teens workbook

Jesus in Blue Jeans: A Practical Guide to Everyday Spirituality

The Power of Positive Prophecy

Teach Your Team to Fish

Grow Something Besides Old

A Personal Note to Graduates

Jesus Life Coach

Jesus Career Counselor

Jesus Entrepreneur

The Four Elements of Success

The Four Elements of Christian Leadership

Made in the USA
Monee, IL
09 May 2023

33151853R00098